What People Are Saying About

A Guide to Angel Communication and Spiritual Laws

A Guide to Angel Communication and Spiritual Laws is a must read for any spiritual seeker looking to connect, and work with Source/God, their guardian angels, and guides. Inspiring, and authentic, Nancy shares her personal adversities, and how they became the springboard for her own personal evolution into spirit. Her letters from St. Gabriel to humanity are especially uplifting and are much needed messages for today.
Jiulio Consiglio, spiritual author & teacher

A useful introduction to access every-day guidance from the spirit world.
Maurice Cotterell, author, engineer & scientist

Nancy shares important spiritual truths that can help everyone in their daily lives. More importantly though, she shares it in a way that is not only interesting, but relatable.
Crystal Pierre, wife, mother & Ragnar Relay Runner

A Guide to Angel Communication and Spiritual Laws

An Angels Connection to God

A Guide to Angel Communication and Spiritual Laws

An Angels Connection to God

Nancy Yearout

6TH
BOOKS

London, UK
Washington, DC, USA

CollectiveInk

First published by Sixth Books, 2025
Sixth Books is an imprint of Collective Ink Ltd.,
Unit 11, Shepperton House, 89 Shepperton Road, London, N1 3DF
office@collectiveinkbooks.com
www.collectiveinkbooks.com
www.6th-books.com

For distributor details and how to order please visit the 'Ordering' section on our website.

Text copyright: Nancy Yearout 2023

ISBN: 978 1 80341 782 0
978 1 80341 789 9 (ebook)
Library of Congress Control Number: 2023918380

A CIP catalogue record for this book is available from the British Library.

Design: Lapiz Digital Services

UK: Printed and bound by CPI Group (UK) Ltd, Croydon, CR0 4YY
Printed in North America by CPI GPS partners

We operate a distinctive and ethical publishing philosophy in all areas of our business, from our global network of authors to production and worldwide distribution.

Guardian Angel Poem

You have a Guardian Angel
Who watches over you
Everywhere you go
And everything you do
Your Angel is ready to help you
Answer any questions you may have and
Comfort you when you're feeling sad
Your guardian Angel loves you unconditionally and
guides you through your life
Get to know your Angel
it will change your life!
Love Nancy

Contents

Previous Books

Wake Up! The Universe Is Speaking to You

987-0-692-79277-3, 978-887-1533383

This book is dedicated to all people who are searching for fulfillment and love in their heart and soul. This is for anyone who is ready to create a reality full of connection, peace, prosperity, joy, and love with Spirit/ God and the Angels.
To my grandchildren Bennett, Isabelle and Xander, my hope is that you will continue my work to help humanity in your lifetimes as you are all three intelligent, beautiful souls I know will make a positive difference. Please know that I love you to the stars and beyond!

Love Nancy

Preface

Humanity is waking up and searching for the answers to why we are here. What is our purpose? How can we understand what our mission is?

Being a seeker myself, I have used my voice interviewing extraordinary guests on my podcast "High Road to Humanity" for years and have witnessed many of these universal and energetic principles spoken about that I am about to share with you. These guidelines have been presented in many ways, yet always the same messages are delivered. These principles have been around for thousands of years but seem forgotten in today's societies.

As an Angel communicator and intuitive, I have always felt that we are not taught how the universal energy works or told how to work with it to manifest our reality and connect to Spirit/God Energy. We are never told that we are energetic beings with energy centers. There is an inquisitive yearning, perhaps now more than ever to understand as so many seek the truth to find answers along with love and fulfillment. My hope is that this information will help many, many people!

This is why it is imperative that we all understand how the universe operates, how the energy flows, and that we can connect to Source Energy, Spirit/God. It is also important to know that we all have a Guardian Angel with whom we can connect with and receive guidance from.

At the end of the book are Archangel Gabriel's messages to humanity that I have channeled. Messages to uplift humanity! These messages are intended to bring you comfort and hope.

My heart-felt aspiration is to share with humanity how to connect with Source Energy, Spirit/ God and Goddess Energy and how to connect to their Guardian Angel. Connecting will make the world a better place for all of humanity. I am speaking and conducting workshops, teaching classes on spiritual law, and how to connect to Spirit/God, the earth's energies, and your Guardian Angel.

Foreword

A Guide to Angel Communication Using Spiritual Law, was written for the masses with the intention of connecting people to Spirit/God Energy and their Guardian Angel. As an Angel communicator, I know that the Divine spark that lies within our soul is the connection that brings the energy of love, joy, peace, and harmony into our lives. The information provided shares step-by-step guidance on how to connect with Spirit/God Energy and your Guardian Angel through the understanding of spiritual laws. The eleven spiritual laws are expanded upon to give the reader a better understanding of how to put the information into practical use. When you know how the universal energy flows you can work with it and not push against it. I tell my story of life lessons learned on my journey and how I became an angel communicator. I teach the reader how to connect with their own Guardian Angel for guidance and support. It is comforting to know that your Angel has your back. In the last section of the book, I reveal Archangel Gabriel's messages to humanity and share these channeled messages with humanity. This is information that is meant to uplift humanity and bring about love and kindness, compassion, connection and hope back into the world.

Acknowledgments

I would like to acknowledge and thank my Guardian Angel who has been by my side through good times and tough times and stands right next to me to guide me along my path in life with love and support. To Spirit/God and the Goddess for showering me with light and loving me and guiding me throughout my life and for teaching me how to connect to the vibration of light and love. Thank you to the hundreds of guests who have put themselves out there and appeared on my show to tell their stories and to share their wisdom with all of humanity. And to Gavin Davies for believing in me and my mission to enlighten humanity.

Introduction

I am writing these words for all the people who are searching for answers. For those seekers of the truth, looking to be fulfilled with peace and love within their hearts and souls. I am writing this because I feel a deep yearning inside my own heart and soul to bring to the forefront what I have discovered and share it with you. Connecting to Spirit/God will bring you amazing rewards. Your health will be better, your energy level will increase, your heart will be full, and your soul will be at peace. Connecting to your Guardian Angel is also a game changer as you have a friend who is by your side nudging you to live your best life. Regardless of your spiritual and religious beliefs, I pray that this information will resonate with you and bring you peace and love and leave you with comfort and hope.

We are amazing human beings who do not realize our power. We all have a spark of Spirit/God within us and possess the ability to create a beautiful life for ourselves. As we ascend to a higher state of consciousness, we will realize more of our abilities. As each person wakes up, they will become aware of their gifts. Our intuition is becoming more heightened, and our manifestations are materializing quickly. To be here in a body on the earth right now is exciting and scary, yet an amazing time to be alive and to see humanity shift to a higher, loving frequency.

As humanity evolves, we all must have faith and believe that a peaceful earth is possible. Just the act of visualizing heaven on earth will speed up the process and create it! Project your good energy out to the universe and let that positive energy rain back on you.

This is why it is imperative that we all understand how the universe operates and how the energy flows. My heartfelt aspiration is to share with humanity how to connect with the energy of the Holy Spirit and how to connect to their Guardian Angel. As we connect to the love vibration, the world will be a better place for all of humanity. Blessings to all.

Love, Nancy

Section One

Navigating Life Using Spiritual Law and Angelic Guidance

I feel most people would like to know how to navigate through life's twists and turns a bit more easily, so I come to you now with an abundance of wisdom to bring forth an understanding of universal law. This wisdom will help you discover how the universe operates and thereby assist you in making your journey much smoother. It will also provide the foundation to connecting to Spirit/God and your Guardian Angel.

When we don't know how the universe works and are not able to stay in the flow of things, we often run into obstacles and challenges and become frustrated about why we are here and what our life's purpose is.

Many of you have come to understand that you have chosen to be here currently on the earth. We all have a role to play in the ascension process as we rise to a new and higher state of consciousness. Even though we may go through difficult times, as our lives are not always rosy, I do feel the energy shifting to a more uplifting and positive vibration. More people are connecting and becoming compassionate and loving towards each other and themselves.

Each of us has a special life purpose, our unique gift for humanity's growth. If you have not found your life purpose yet, it is the one thing that has been nudging you and nagging at you from behind the scenes to go for it! What have you always wanted to be or do since your childhood days? That is always the thing that will bring you the most joy and the prosperity will flow. I have realized that we are aware of our life's plan when we are children and still remember it and begin early trying to act it out. Guys who played with trucks often grow up to drive big rigs or work in the construction industry. Girls who grew up singing and performing and followed their dreams are working in some aspect of the performing arts. If you take a moment now and think back to when you were a child and what you played with or acted out, see how it relates to the career path you have chosen. If you do what you love, you will always be happy, and it will not feel like work. Unfortunately, we live in a society that tells us what industry we should go into to make the most money instead of encouraging people to follow their dreams and understand that the universe will take care of the rest, and money will flow to you easily as your vibration will be high.

The information that I am sharing with you is a treasure map to happiness and fulfillment, love and understanding, compassion and kindness. My hope is for all of us to find the treasure that lies within ourselves and to connect with the spark of Spirit/God in our hearts.

There is much anger, fear, and unrest on our planet. This has caused many people to be fearful and lose hope. I want you to know that there is hope for all of humanity as the light will win this battle against evil.

It saddens me as I write but at this time, wars are being fought in Ukraine, Israel, and Palestine. The evil is giving humanity a good fight.

There is no need to be fearful for all who connect with the divine light energy are at peace within themselves, and know we are eternal beings.

The emotion of fear was created by man or an entity but not by Spirit/God, the radiant one, who loves all of us unconditionally and wants us to be happy. Spirit/God desires to have a relationship with us and it is comforting when you do. It's trusting and having faith in a loving, powerful energy bigger than yourself that will bring comfort to your soul. I will say this amazing energy of love will change one's life.

We the people can create the life we desire. It is important to stay in the present moment and not refer to past rough roads. We all make mistakes as we travel along our path in life. Please don't get frustrated as life is not perfect. Life is not supposed to be, for if it were perfect, we would not learn anything and what would be the point of us living and experiencing life?

We are here to experience life in these precious bodies and to learn how to elevate our souls to a higher level of understanding of connection, compassion, and love.

We are here to elevate our souls to the light of love, and some say upon completion, return to where we originated from, Spirit/God the Source, the love energy of the radiant one who created us and loves us all unconditionally.

This book is intended to give you, the reader, a better understanding of why we are here, where we are headed, and how to connect with the love of Spirit/God and the Angelic realm while living life here on earth.

The Angels are God/Spirit helpers and can be great friends who will stand by your side.

It is important for all of humanity to understand spiritual law and how it works. Knowing how the universe operates and that we all have our own Guardian Angel is a game changer.

"If you don't know where you are going, you might wind up someplace else."
Yogi Berra

Our Guardian Angel watches over us and guides us if we ask. Knowing that we are not alone gives us the ability to create the life we desire with confidence. How can you live the life of your dreams if you don't know how the universe is set up? And isn't it comforting and empowering to know you have an Angel by your side helping you out?

3

I feel most of this knowledge has been hidden from the collective to control humanity. It is sad to say that a few seeking to control the masses for reasons of power and pure greed have known how the world turns but have not shared this knowledge, but now more of us are seeing the truth and are understanding how the universe works.

The good news is that humanity is waking up! We are now in the Age of Aquarius!

My goal is to paint a clear picture of how the universe works sharing spiritual law which will assist you in connecting with your Guardian Angel.

Universal law may provide you with a new perspective on how to work with it to benefit yourself and others. You will discover you can work with the energy of the universe to create your reality as you choose. We are all creators and have the creative ability from the Divine Source in each one of us.

These spiritual principles are things that I had to understand and practice to connect to God/Source and to my own Guardian Angel. One of the first principles I learned was the power of the spoken word and the manifesting ability of what you say to others and about yourself.

"In the beginning, there was the Word, and the Word was with God and the Word was God". St. John 1:1 NIV Study Bible

Section Two

My Angelic Story

"Earth Angels shine their light out in the world bringing joy and hope and love to humanity."
Nancy Yearout

Becoming acquainted with the Angelic realm has been a gradual one for me.

I have always felt different from others and have felt out of place my entire life. To give you a glimpse into my reality, all I daydreamed about at an early age was becoming an Angel. The vision drifted as I grew older, but I do remember wanting to be an Angel as a child. Now what little kid dreams of being an Angel who flies around helping people?

Growing up in rural Ohio on a farm was a good thing for me as nature seemed to be my savior. I ran around barefoot on our farm and picked blackberries in the woods, found kittens in our barn, nearly every year skated on our pond in the winter, and even went frog gigging with my Uncle Donald in the summertime. We grew up playing baseball, and badminton, and croquet on many acres of mowed green grass.

My first Angelic experience was at the age of 9 or 10 when I was an Angel for the Halloween Parade in our small town. My father is owed most of the credit for the designing of my wings with coat hangers, trimmed in gold garland with a halo above my hair.

My Angel costume went over big at the Halloween Parade in our small town where my portrayal was awarded the first prize! I have always wondered if my dad had a feeling about my Angelic vibe.

My mother was not so kind, and in fact, you may refer to her as a harsh person. She is what today we refer to as a narcissist. It has taken me many years to understand the narcissistic personality. It's not an exaggeration to say she was as cruel and conniving as Cruella de Vil.

It seemed that my mother was always cooking or washing clothes or attending one of her clubs. I recall that she belonged to the Order of the Eastern Star and was the President of the PTA at my school. Although she was very active in the community, she never spent any time with me. My mother rarely kissed me, and never hugged me as a child nor as an adult. Because of the lack of affection, I waited daily for my father to return home from work as he always had a hug and kiss for me at the door.

I know they say we pick our parents and I believe we do, but for me difficult lessons have been learned living with a narcissistic mother. In her defense, she probably did not know what to do with a psychic angelic soul as a daughter who spoke her mind. I believe life was a challenge for the both of us. She did however teach me proper manners, how to dress appropriately, to speak properly, and how to cook. I am a fantastic cook, but my mother was better.

School came easy for me, and I always did well but I did not like going. Many of the kids were mean to each other and at the time I did not understand their motives. I was grateful to have had several girlfriends and boyfriends which made school more bearable, but I felt like I just wanted to get through it and get on with my life. So much of what they were teaching did not interest me. My search was for love and affection and success!

My path has had many challenges thrown in my way, as all of us have, however, it is my experiences that have gotten me to where I am today and created the person I am now. Here are the events that I believe changed my life for the better: a narcissistic mother, marriage to the wrong people, raising children as a single mother, divorce, becoming the breadwinner, marriage to the wrong person who was a narcissist, divorce, single mom, marriage to another narcissist, divorce, single mom, breadwinner, caregiver, motivator, being both parents, successful career, financially successful, marriage to a liar, betrayal, starting over, financial struggles, becoming a new person, knowing I am an Angelic soul, and taking back my Power!

Well, that just sums it up in a nutshell, doesn't it? It has been a long road and often bumpy but rarely a dull moment. I have come to realize that when you're an Angelic soul, you think everyone is honest and truthful like you are and it's a surprise to find out that people are not what they seem.

I believe that people are generally good, but that many of us have not taken the time to work on issues that may have occurred in childhood or even past lives to heal and grow. I will give you a brief overview of where I came from.

I married my high school sweetheart at the age of 19, escaping a narcissistic home life and looking for love. I gave birth to our daughter when I was 20. My husband and I were happy and in love with each other and with our child. My husband had joined the army before we were married, and he seemed to enjoy this work, but after a time alcohol became his new friend.

We had moved overseas to Germany where he was born to meet his relatives and to see the sights with our daughter. We were both young and adventurous, so we were excited about our new life together. The fairytale did not last long, and his drinking increased. Before I knew it, my husband was pounding down a liter of hefeweizen, a German style wheat beer at lunchtime. He had inner demons that I now realize were never dealt with. We both had things to work through, although his were a bit more extreme. I recall he left us one weekend to go to Amsterdam to party. After that escape, our relationship went downhill quickly. The alcohol had taken my place. My daughter and I eventually returned to the States, and I filed for divorce.

I have to say on my first husband's behalf that his mother left the family when he was young, and her absence had a huge impact on him, as it would any child who had lost their mother. We were the same as my mom was there but not present, so at a soul level we energetically found one another, both looking for the love that we seemed to be lacking. Regardless of our love for each other and our child, he grew to love alcohol more than the both of us. He passed away from cardiac arrest at the young age of 35. He was a wonderful soul and I think maybe he was not meant for this harsh world we live in.

I have learned that each experience in our lives teaches us a lesson and if you don't learn that lesson the first time, the universe will present it to you again and again until you get it!

Most people do not realize they marry their narcissistic mother or father and if they did, they would cringe, but somewhere deep down in your soul those feelings are striving to be worked out with your new husband or wife. As you may know, like attracts like, for example you attract the person who is on the same vibration as you are at that time. Sidenote: I believe many divorces occur as one of the parties grows at a soul level and the other grows in a different direction or stays the same.

I did marry again and am blessed with a second daughter. My lessons were accumulating, and I was learning that just because you love somebody, and they love you, does not mean it's going to work out. What I have discovered is that you think you know a person and their personality, but everyone shows their best side before marriage. It's when the true person emerges that the bonds of matrimony are tested. Is the strength of your love for each other strong enough to not be broken by the events of life? My answer is yes. Two healthy people can make it. But there are many like me who had to heal to move forward to a healthy relationship with an equally healthy person. You attract your mate energetically.

All of us have an energetic soul that arrived with us at birth. We have energy centers in our bodies that correspond to specific nerve bundles and internal organs. There are seven major chakras or energy centers that run from the top of your head to the base of your spine. I believe that when one of our energy centers is blocked or out of balance, it may cause disease. Know that everything is energy, and your soul is light energy and never dies. If your emotions are out of whack, so are your energy fields. It is important for the body to stay balanced energetically. This energetic balance will assist in good overall health. One of the reasons I am writing this book is to share with you what I wished I had known when I was younger.

My second marriage was supposed to last forever but then real-life stepped in. Everyone has a different work ethic, and my second husband did not have the same work ethic as I had learned growing up. My father worked as an engineer during the week and farmed on the weekends. My new husband's father was killed in Vietnam when he was young, so he did not remember him or have the positive influence of a father figure in his life. He too had a parent that was absent. It is as if the energy of all of us who felt they were missing a parent were drawn to each other. Now I realize years later it was not just a physical attraction, it was also an energetic attraction. Do you see the pattern I was repeating? At the time I did not, but of course now it is as clear as day to me.

All these experiences have made me who I am today, a stronger wiser soul, and while I was learning these life lessons my intuition and empathic abilities were growing stronger.

I felt the need to write about the energy of the spoken word, about affirmations, and how saying them consistently had worked for me as a single mom in the real estate industry. I wanted everyone to know about the power of the spoken word and manifestation. Then I began to realize that manifestation was written about in the Bible in Isaiah 55:11: "so it is my word that goes out from my mouth; it will not return to me empty but will accomplish what I desire and achieve the purpose for which I sent it." With this new awareness more things began connecting as my own abilities were growing stronger. I met other spiritual people and joined a drumming group. I researched many religions and their beliefs as most seekers do. I was fortunate to study with an Aztec healer and learned energy healing. In recent years I have taken the healing with light workshops and have enhanced my knowledge and expertise in energy healing. We all can heal ourselves and learn to run energy to each other to assist in the healing process. As I learned all these new spiritual practices, I was still searching for love. Well, I sent out the love vibration and met the man I thought I would grow old with.

I married again, feeling that he was my soulmate. We were so happy and in love with each other. We decided to travel together as his work took him to surrounding states. When he was working, this gave me the opportunity to write. This was the first time in a long time that I was not the so-called breadwinner and could do what I desired.

I wrote my first book about the energy of faith, love, prayer, water, the spoken word, our thoughts, and more. The title is *Wake Up! The Universe is Speaking to You*. I wrote about the power and energy of the spoken word, visualizations, gratitude, music, a chapter on the energy of numbers, and on Angels of course. I had discovered so much on my journey that I knew had changed my life, and I had to share it with everyone! I learned a few secrets of the universe that had to be revealed.

After the book came out, I felt as if I was not being heard and that my message was not getting out to humanity as I had hoped.

I was a guest on many podcasts speaking about the book, and everyone loved it, but I needed to reach a larger audience.

My intention then and now is to reach the masses with this information.

My marriage did not work out as I had planned. Angel's love everybody and only see the good in those they are in love with. My psychic abilities increased tremendously during this time as I had been connecting with the Source daily for quite a while. It was my empathic abilities that increased and showed me the truth. Being an empath is a blessing but often a curse. One evening while talking to my husband, I saw a dark-haired girl sitting next to him, as plain as day. The energetic imprint was still there when he came home from work and sat on our living room sofa. I was shocked and filled with disbelief and did not want to acknowledge my own gifts. I called every intuitive I could find hoping I was just off my rocker. They all had the same answer. I was correct. He was seeing someone else. I had never been betrayed before and honestly, the energy of betrayal is intense. I realized that I had married a narcissist and as soon as I began writing and focusing my attention on myself, my husband found someone who would focus on him, but not always for the right reasons.

I knew we had grown apart and tried a marriage counselor, but counseling did not work and neither did his untruths.

I knew he would never be honest with me so I could never trust him, and I believed he would do it again. So, I left and started over, again.

It took many years to recover as Angel's love deeply and even though I knew he was not the one for me, I would have stayed with him and honored our marriage and tried to make it work, but infidelity was the final straw for me.

I now realize what a blessing this lesson was. It forced me to go within and work on myself. I had to come to terms with the root of the problem, my mother, and her narcissistic behavior. I had to forgive her, forgive myself, and move forward. I did inner child work and am so glad I did it! I recommend everyone handle your childhood issues. We all have something to address it seems. Every one of us has had experiences in our childhood that we carry with us into adulthood, that often need to be released for us to move forward in our lives. I recommend everyone get to know their inner child, that little one that may be looking for love, approval, and attention. Connect with your inner child and you will feel complete in many ways. The work does pay off in a big way creating a new life of joy, freedom, and love for yourself and for others.

Section Three

How to Connect to Source the Holy Spirit Energy

The Bible, the Bhagavad Gita, and the Upanishads all contain stories of ancient times, full of lessons and truths written as guidelines for humanity. I am sure there are books that have been left out of the Bible and others and the interpretation of many passages have been defined improperly but the intent is to guide us through life. No matter what your beliefs are or what religion or denomination you connect with, if any, this wisdom, and guidance stands true today as Holy Divine guidance is desperately needed now.

Spirit/ God and the Goddess, the light loves all of us and desires us to be happy and joyful, prosperous, and peaceful, Spirit/God and the Goddess gave us life and encourages us to use our amazing minds, our loving hearts, and our compassionate souls to create good, not evil.

Understanding the energetic operation of the universe is eye-opening. Everything is energy, and we should be taught these principles when we are children. My connection with the Divine Source has shown me first-hand how powerful this connection is that I am about to reveal.

My goal is to guide you to connect to Spirit/God, Goddess Energy and to your own personal Guardian Angel. Many of you know some of these principles already and my hope is you will discover new tools and techniques.

My passion is to teach all of humanity love and ultimately to teach people how to connect to Spirit/God and their Angel.

"As the world becomes a more digital place, we cannot forget about the human connection."
Adam Neumann

Let us begin by connecting to Source Energy.

Connecting to this frequency is as simple and easy as connecting to the internet but in a reverent way. For me connecting is a holy and sacred practice. I light a white candle to signify reverence for the Divine Source Energy, often called the Holy Spirit and to show my appreciation for my life and say the Lord's Prayer out loud. You can choose to do the same if this resonates with you, but it is important to set your intention. Spirt/God wants to have a relationship with you. The Spirit/God knows that we are all individually unique and important ... Some people pray and some of us journal. Some of us have conversations with Spirit/God. I am nudging anyone who has not established a relationship with Spirit/God and the Goddess to begin now. It may feel awkward at first but have faith, believe that you are being heard, because you are.

To connect with Spirit/God and Mother Earth/Gaia you will want to begin by sitting in a comfortable chair with your feet flat on the ground.

1. The first thing you will do is to ground your energy. This means that you are to connect with the earth energies beneath your feet. There are many ways to ground yourself, for example walking outside barefoot on the earth and picking up the healing vibrations. Feeling these earth vibrations through the bottoms of your feet is a wonderful and natural way to feel connected to the earth. Or you can visualize roots coming out of the bottom of your feet and your tailbone rooting down and anchoring into the earth itself. Visualize the roots going down until

you feel, see, or know you are connecting to the light from Mother Earth. Once you feel, sense or see the light from below you are now connected to the healing energies of the earth. The next step is to connect to Spirit/God.

2. To connect to the Holy Spirit energy, you will want to be in a comfortable position, preferably sitting. Many people will light a white candle in reverence before connecting with the Divine Source and it is important to say a prayer. Here is a prayer that I say before connecting: May the Light of God surround us, may the presence of God watch over us, wherever we are God is. May the love of God enfold us, may the light of God surround us, may the power of God protect us, may the presence of God watch over us wherever you are God is.

Now close your eyes and let all of the noise from the outside world disappear. Visualize pure white light coming down from about your head, from the heavenly realms, entering through your crown and enveloping down through your face and throat, down your neck, throughout your chest, and down the torso. Visualize the pure white light in your mind's eye pouring into your abdomen and down through your entire body, out your arms, out your fingers, down your legs, and out through your feet. You have brought in the heavenly pure light of love from above and have run it through your entire body and you have brought up the light of Mother Earth from below to ground the energies. You are now energetically connected to Spirit/God and grounded in the light and love of Mother Earth, which is a joyful state of being. It only takes a few minutes to connect in the morning to the Holy Spirit then you are connected all day. You can connect at any time that feels right for you.

You must do what is comfortable for you, but you get the basic idea. This does not take long. You can also bring in any color of light that feels good to you to enhance the healing of the body, mind, and soul. After bringing in the white light, ask Spirit/God, "What color do I need today?" and then listen. You can ask Spirit/God and the Goddess, "What messages do you have for me today?" and just listen for the answer. The answers will come immediately with no hesitation that is how you know you are receiving the information and it's not your own thoughts. The messages are received instantly, there is no hesitation.

Connecting to the Holy Spirit and the Lively Earth regenerates our energy fields. Connecting, I believe, was something people did as they understood the benefits. Once you begin connecting this is a practice that is easy to get addicted to as you feel so good. It's addictive!

In return, say what you are grateful for. Most of us, if truth be told are grateful to have a warm bed, food to eat, a nice home to live in. These are blessings. The gift of good health is also a huge blessing to be grateful for as there are many who are not so fortunate. We can also express gratitude for our pets that we love and care for as they stand by us and love us unconditionally.

There are many benefits to connecting to Spirit. You receive healing energy when you connect to Source which keeps your energy fields in balance. You will begin to feel more love in your heart and joy in your soul. Your energetic vibration will rise, and you will be a more joyful person. You will find yourself humming and smiling more often. You become the light that goes out into the world to shine. The vibration of light alone heals people as you meet them.

Section Four

The Angels

"May you believe that you always have an angel by your side."
Unknown author

Although much has been written about Angels throughout time, we don't seem to acknowledge their presence. They are mentioned nearly 300 times throughout the Bible. Archangels Michael, Gabriel, and Uriel are mentioned by name. There are many documented accounts of Angels existing throughout history. Numerous paintings have been created depicting many different Angelic beings. We all have a Guardian Angel who helps us with our life's challenges. Your Guardian Angel is with you when you are born and is present when your body dies to assist your soul to heaven. I don't recall when I began asking the Angels for their help but when I did, it seemed that they were always ready to assist me. This may be a new concept for you, so try to be open-minded. When you ask for their assistance with pure intent, they help you every time. It's truly amazing. I have many stories about Angels and how I came to believe.

For he will command his angels concerning you to guard you in all your ways. Psalm 91: 11

Angels play an important role in carrying Spirit/ God's plan for us and our world. This passage refers to Angels.

Are not Angels ministering spirits sent to serve those who will inherit salvation? Hebrews 1:14

This may come as a surprise for many of you, but I am revealing that there are many Angelic souls who have incarnated into human form to be here currently on Earth to assist in raising the vibration on the planet and that is one of the reasons that I am writing this book. The first is to bring forth information that will increase love and peace for all of humanity, and the animal and plant kingdoms. The second is to bring Archangel Gabriel's messages to the masses as he is God's messenger and humanity will benefit from his words. The third reason is for all the Angelic and elemental souls who are here on this planet right now living in human bodies helping to uplift humanity with their light and love. The earth has not been an easy place to live for empathic souls but necessary for us to be present and to spread love and compassion to the people and the planet.

These higher vibrational souls spread the energetic vibration of light, love, and kindness to humanity just by being present with their high vibrational energy.

What I have learned over time is that there are various types of Angelic beings who are the Creator's helpers. Angels each have a specialty. Each has a unique talent, just as we do.

St. Gabriel is the messenger Angel, while Archangel Raphael is the healing Angel. His name means "God has healed." Archangel Michael is said to be the chief of the Angels and Archangels and he is the guardian prince of Israel who is responsible for its care. He is known as the warrior Angel. He watches over me. He has taught me how to protect myself from negative energies or entities that do not belong in my energy field. Just as we all have our own special talents, so do the Angels.

We all can call in specific Angels to help us in our lives to assist us with specific requests. I will talk more about this later in the book.

You can communicate with Angels like I do. The Angels are God's helpers. They are ready to guide us when we call on them. You can speak to the Angels as you would a friend. We can ask for their assistance when we need it, but the key is you must ask.

Know that any request must be for your highest good as well as anyone else involved. The Angels will help with even the smallest things. If you are late for work, ask that the Angels get you there on time. I have done this for years and it always works. I began to realize that they can manipulate time. I request that they watch over my children and grandchildren when I feel they need guidance and support. I call on them and ask that they watch over my travels, as they are God's helpers. The key is to just ask. Do not be afraid or think that your request is not important. All requests are heard and answered. It may not always be in your time frame, but it will be in God's.

Do not forget to show hospitality to strangers, for by so doing some people have shown. hospitality to Angels without knowing it. Hebrews 13: 2

Our prayers are received and heard in heaven. I interviewed a guest on my show who came from a religious family and had a near-death experience. When she was out of her body, she saw the prayers for her floating up to heaven and assured me and the audience that our prayers are received and heard. Angels will take on different forms to assist you in life. This I know has happened to me a couple times that I am aware of. When my kids were little, I worked many hours as a single mom. I would pick up the girls from their after-school program, cook dinner, deal with homework, give baths, and send them off to bed. I was often exhausted at the end of the workday. One evening I was so tired I fell asleep on the couch after putting the girls to bed. I was not aware that I had forgotten to lock my front door. This was not like me at all. Suddenly I was awoken by a very loud pounding on the front door. Startled by the loud banging,

I jumped up and quickly answered it. There was an older lady standing there with piercing blue eyes. I wasn't completely awake, so I am not even sure what she said to me, "wrong home," or something to that effect. I do remember however that she had the strangest look in her piercing blue eyes, like, "Lock your door, girlfriend." It was the most bizarre thing. I locked and bolted the door behind her and wondered, "Who was that?" Then I thought, someone wanted to make sure we were safe and for me to lock the front door. Thinking back, I realized she must have been an Angel looking after us, as I never saw this woman again. As we travel along our path in life it gets winding and twisty at times.

It seems that life will go along smoothly for a while and then suddenly, without warning, a new bump will appear on the road. Most of these little bumps are tolerable but the big bumps can be debilitating.

Most people realize that life is a series of ups and downs. It does not matter if you are young, old, rich, poor, man or woman, healthy or sickly, the ups and downs cannot be avoided. This is how we learn life's lessons, universal law. It is how we handle the bumps in the road and the choices we make that determine our next steps.

Do you recognize that the universe is speaking to you? Are you aware of the message being conveyed when your path becomes rocky?

I am here to confirm that universal law is real. My discovery occurred over time as I became aware that when I did not learn the lesson the first time, the universe placed in front of me the same set of circumstances in my path again. It was a do-over!

The universal powers that be orchestrate a repeat of the event with another person, but with the same scenario. After a couple of times of this you begin to see a pattern and realize this is how the universal energy works and the universe is looking for a new outcome. You must live it again and do it over until you get it right. Or you can choose to continue doing the same thing over and over and never get the lesson in that area of your life.

So, does our path become smoother as our lessons are learned?

The answer is yes. Once you understand how the universal law works, you can navigate the bumps much easier. This is why I have shown up today to share what I have discovered with you.

Personally, it has taken many years of lessons repeated, reading books, conversations with the experts, consistent meditation, connecting with my Angels and the Divine Source for me to recognize how the universe works and to make this change in consciousness.

Today, I feel balanced and fulfilled not looking for something outside of myself to make me feel good about myself or my life choices. I have shifted my energy to a more loving and positive vibration. The effort has paid off tenfold. The connection that I have with God, the Divine Source, has created balance and fulfillment. The search for love had ended when I found the love of God. I can honestly say that today, right now, is the happiest I have ever felt. To be completely honest with you, it has taken me many years to be my authentic self and say, "I am a psychic empath," out loud and be proud of who I am. I am an intuitive and what many refer to as an empath with the gifts of claircognizance (clear knowing), clairsentience (clear physical feeling), and clairsalience (clear smelling), some clairvoyance (clear seeing). I am an Angel communicator and an energy healer. My Angelic journey began by experimenting with energy and the concept of asking for sales when I was in the real estate business many years ago. I was a single mom and needed to draw in business to myself so I could pay the bills. I learned how to draw things to myself with affirmations and visualizations. This instruction came from Naomi Kreuger, my first teacher. I am forever grateful for her guidance and love.

She taught me how to draw things to myself and in this case business.

The other important thing she taught me was to have faith, faith in God, a higher power. Naomi told me how faith works. She gave me a little porcelain figurine that reads "Faith Works," and the statue is with me today. She sits on my kitchen windowsill as a reminder of my friend Naomi and to have faith that there is a higher power, a Creator God, a Divine Source that loves us all unconditionally. Faith is not easy to learn but when you do it, its life changing. It's believing in a good energy that you cannot see, a love force. Once you put your intention out to the universe and ask for what you desire (knowing that you will receive that or something better) and see positive results, there becomes an understanding of how the universe is structured. It's like magic. I ask the universe for a red dress that's on sale in my size and I walk into the store and find the perfect red dress marked down. After a while, you realize this stuff truly works and these are the same principles that Jesus was explaining to us in the Bible many times. You reap what you sow; knock and the door shall be opened. Meaning — ask and believe and you will receive what you are looking for or something better. The same concept goes for having faith. Once you have faith, *true faith* that there is a higher power looking out for your best interest and that loves you unconditionally like a parent loves a child, then faith is believed and understood. I had heard about conversing with the Angels, so the next step on my path was asking the Angels for their assistance. I understood that they were God's helpers but was quite naive when I first began conversing. I have always felt a connection to the Angelic realm. I am sure many people say this, but I feel this connection in my heart and soul. I have pictures and statues of Angels throughout my home and always have and I read many books about the Angels. The book that made the most impact on me many years ago was

Hiring the Heavens by Jean Slatter. Jean confirmed what I felt to be true about working with the Angels, but she took it a step further by explaining that they all had a specialty like we do. I was blessed to meet Jean years later as she agreed to be a guest on my show. What a wonderful soul to have brought forth this information about the Angels! We can all work with the Angelic realm. We just must ask.

The English word "angel" comes from the Greek word angelos which means to send. The corresponding Hebrew word is malach (malachim in the plural) which means messenger. In both cases it is a "job description" rather than a description of their essence or nature. from firmisrael.org.

One of the first Angels that I communicated with was St. Michael the Archangel. St. Michael is near and dear to my heart. I have always felt an attachment to him. I use his blue flame sword of truth for protection and know many who do the same. I am extremely fond of Archangel Michael and feel a soul connection to his energy. He is known as the warrior Angel according to the Bible. I always say I am a warrior because I have hung in there through good times and bad and I still have a good fighting spirit, with love in my heart. This is why I can relate to him as I feel I am a warrior, fighting for humanity. This verse from Revelations clearly demonstrates to the world what a warrior Archangel Michael is. Since I feel most comfortable with Michael, I call on him for protection and guidance if I am going to be in a tough situation.

This verse from Revelations clearly demonstrates to the world what a warrior Archangel Michael is. Since I feel most comfortable with Michael, I call on him for protection and guidance if I am going to be in a tough situation and suggest that you call on him also. The Angels are always willing to help us.

7 Then war broke out in heaven. Michael and his angels fought against the dragon and the dragon, and his angels fought back. 8 But he was not strong enough and they lost their place in heaven. 9 The great dragon was hurled down — that ancient serpent called the devil, or Satan, who leads the whole world astray. He was hurled to the earth, and his angels with him."

Revelations 12:7–9

The Angels that work with Archangel Michael are of the Christ light but do know as the Bible reveals in Revelations that the dark angles reside here on earth too. This is why, when you are calling the Angels, you must be specific of who and what you are calling in. Ask to receive messages from the angels who are Divine and Holy and are of the light of Spirit/God.

One morning I was driving to work, and I felt like I needed protection from all the negativity in the world. I called on Archangel Michael and asked him to watch over me. It had not been 5 or 10 minutes since I asked out loud for extra protection that I felt my car come to a screeching halt. The car in front of me had stopped abruptly and I did not see the car's brake lights go on. The car stopped before I could even put my foot on the pedal. I was rattled, but everything was fine. I thought, "What just happened to me? My prayer was answered, and that quickly?" It startled me. The Angels stopped my car! It was St. Michael if truth be told.

Now would be a good time to explain how I began communicating with my personal Angel. It all began after writing my first book *Wake Up! The Universe is Speaking to You.* I was interviewed on many podcasts promoting my book and really enjoyed the energy and the exchange of information that was being brought forth by so many wise people, so in January 2019 I launched my first show, *High Road to Humanity.* Meeting many people who were also empaths and energy healers was comforting. I learned to meditate from reading so many books on meditation. You tend to take up the practice after realizing the amazing results. The guests who I have interviewed have taught me so much more than I knew before. Several have recognized my Angelic vibration which confirmed what I thought I knew. I have chosen to be here to help humanity learn about love and compassion. My Guardian Angel stands right next to me. Once I acknowledged her presence and began communicating with her, I felt great comfort knowing she is by my side looking out for me. It took me a while to trust the information that she told me telepathically, but I now call on her when I'm having a tough day or if I just have a question for myself or another person who is looking for guidance. When we trust in God, our guides, and Angels, we are connecting to the spiritual side of ourselves.

Accounts of incarnated Angels date back to Biblical times, as the Apostle Paul reminds us in Hebrews.9:5. Spirit/God would like me to talk about the Cherubim. The Cherubim are misunderstood. Cherubim are God's friends and protectors thus signifying their importance in the heavenly realms. It is said in the Bible in the book of Ephesians 1:21 and Colossians 1:16 that there are three hierarchies of Angels; the first is the Seraphim, Cherubin, and Throne Seraphim. These are the angels that are the closest to Spirit/God. According to Abrahamic religions the angels closest to Spirit/God can look at him directly. The Cherubim are wise and have been painted blue with four wings with eyes.

Cherubim are mentioned many times in the Bible by various authors but first Genesis.

After he drove the man out, he placed on the east side of the Garden of Eden cherubim and a flaming sword flashing back and forth to guard the way to the tree of life. Genesis 3:24

The Book of Ezekiel speaks more in depth about the Cherubim. Here are a few verses that describe the Cherubim from the Bible.

Ezekiel Chapter 10 1–22

1. *I looked, and I saw the likeness of a throne of sapphire[1] above the expanse that was over the heads of the cherubim.*
2. *The LORD said to the man clothed in linen, "Go in among the wheels beneath the cherubim. Fill your hands with burning coals from among the cherubim and scatter them over the city." And as I watched, he went in.*
3. *Now the cherubim were standing on the south side of the temple when the man went in, and a cloud filled the inner court.*
4. *Then the glory of the LORD rose from above the cherubim and moved to the threshold of the temple. The cloud filled the temple, and the court was full of the radiance of the glory of the LORD.*
5. *The sound of the wings of the cherubim could be heard as far away as the outer court, like the voice of God Almighty when he speaks.*
6. *When the LORD commanded the man in linen, "Take fire from among the wheels, from. among the cherubim," the man went in and stood beside a wheel.*
7. *Then one of the cherubim reached out his hand to the fire that was among them. He took up some of it and put it into the hands of the man in linen, who took it and went out.*
8. *(Under the wings of the cherubim could be seen what looked like the hands of a man.)*
9. *I looked, and I saw beside the cherubim four wheels, one beside each of the cherubim; the wheels sparkled like chrysolite.*
10. *As for their appearance, the four of them looked alike; each was like a wheel intersecting a wheel.*
11. *As they moved; they would go in any one of the four directions the cherubim faced the wheels did not turn about as the*

cherubim went. The cherubim went in whatever direction the head faced, without turning as they went.

12. *Their entire bodies, including their backs, their hands, and their wings, were completely full of eyes, as were their four wheels.*

13. *heard the wheels being called "the whirling wheels."*

14. *Each of the cherubim had four faces: One face was that of a cherub, the second the face of a man, the third the face of a lion, and the fourth the face of an eagle.*

15. *Then the cherubim rose upward. These were the living creatures I had seen by the Kebar River.*

16. *When the cherubim moved, the wheels beside them moved; and when the cherubim spread their wings to rise from the ground, the wheels did not leave their side.*

17. *When the cherubim stood still, they also stood still; and when the cherubim rose, they rose with them, because the spirit of the living creatures was in them.*

18. *Then the glory of the LORD departed from over the threshold of the temple and stopped above the cherubim.*

19. *While I watched, the cherubim spread their wings and rose from the ground, and as they went, the wheels went with them. They stopped at the entrance to the east gate.*

20. *These were the living creatures I had seen beneath the God of Israel by the Kebar River, and I realized that they were cherubim.*

21. *Each had four faces and four wings, and under their wings was what looked like the hands of a man.*

22. *Their faces had the same appearance as those I had seen by the Kebar River. Each one went straight ahead.*

The effort has paid off tenfold. The connection that I have with God, the Divine Source, has created balance and fulfillment. The search for love had ended when I found the love of God.

There are many empaths on the earth plain currently to bring more empathy to our world. There are many Angelic souls who have chosen to incarnate currently as well as elementals. So many humans are aware of their abilities but are afraid to say who they truly are as they feel they will be judged. I am no different. My psychic abilities have always been strong but when I first spoke of my connection to the Angelic realm and to Spirit/God many who were close to me rolled their eyes and did not believe. Judgment is something that is spoken of much in the Bible, Jesus said.

"Do not judge, or you too will be judged."Matthew 7

Many people are afraid to be their true authentic selves because of the judgment they will receive from their family, friends, and even strangers.

Judgment has become a large part of our society and must be reversed. You have no idea what another person has experienced in their lifetime and cannot judge their path. We are reminded of this in the Book of James from the Holy Bible.

Do not speak evil against one another, brothers. The one who speaks about a brother or judges his brother, speaks evil against the law and judges the law. But if you judge the law, you are not a doer of the law but a judge. There is only one lawgiver and judge, he who is able to save and destroy. But who are you to judge your neighbor? James 4:11–12

In the above passage, James is telling us that the only judge is Source, God our Creator, the one of light, the one who loves all of us unconditionally.

I have searched for love without judgment my entire life. I have come to realize that true unconditional love is not found with shiny objects or other people. True love comes by having a relationship with the Source, with God Almighty. I found love when I connected to the love energy of the Divine Source, God.

The effort has paid off tenfold. The connection that I have with God, the Divine Source, has created balance and fulfillment. The search for love ended when I found the love of God.

How to Connect with Your Guardian Angel

Connecting with your Guardian Angel is a magical experience. You can connect with your Guardian Angel and ask anything that you would like to know. When you ask your Angel a question the message will arrive quickly with no hesitation, that is how you know the message is from your Angel and not your own thoughts.

The process of connection takes no more than 10–15 minutes depending upon how long you choose to quiet your mind and listen to the messages.

"Our Guardian Angels are closer to us than anything except the love of God."
Eileen Elias Freeman

There are many wonderful books in which you can read about Angels but let's begin by recognizing that the angels are with us. These Angelic beings are the Divine helpers to guide us. The Angels want to have a relationship with us and you can start by acknowledging their presence. You will be amazed by the assistance they will give to you when you request their help.

The Guardian Angels are mentioned in *Henry V Act 1 Scene 2,* as the Bishop of Canterbury addresses the king and states, "God and his Angels guard your sacred throne, and make you long become it!" In modern times the Angels are spoken of in new ways as motorists refer to the "Traffic Angels" as there have been so many motorists helped by angels, they have been given this name.

Here are the steps to follow to communicate with your Guardian Angel.

1. The first step is to say a prayer. You will request to speak with your Guardian Angel who is of the light of Spirit/ God. It is important that you only call in what is Holy and Divine. Next acknowledge your Angel is with you. Your Angel has been with you from birth and will be delighted that you are acknowledging their presence. Tell them what feels comfortable for you but let them know that you would like to communicate with them. You can even ask for a sign that they are with you. Often after connecting you may see a Cardinal or find a feather. These are signs that the Angels will leave for you. There are many signs that your Angel will send to get your attention and confirm their presence.

2. The Second step is to ask your guardian Angel a simple question, such as what should I have for breakfast? Or which road is best to take today on my travels? Ask and then listen. Your message will come swiftly. This will help you recognize the difference between your Angel's guidance and your own thoughts. For example, in the morning as I begin my day, I may ask my Angel what do I need to know today? My angel provides me with any information to help make my life easier. Now if by chance you receive negative information, you are not talking to your Angel. The angels, however brutally honest, are not negative, mean, or cruel. The Angels are loving and kind entities but remember truthful to a fault. Your Angel wants you to communicate and cannot help you unless you ask, as all humans have free will and must choose the path of connection.

3. The third step is to ask your Angel their name. These Angelic beings have long names that may be difficult for you to pronounce at first. You may want to shorten it to make it easier to say. My Angel's name is long, so I shortened it and she's good with that. I see my guardian

angel as a female Angel, but you may see yours as a male or having no sex at all, just a loving friend that watches out for your best interest and guides you along your way. Begin to use your Angel's name when you are asking for direction or advice. When you connect with your Angel, it's as if you have a new friend who has your back, an assistant to help you through life's ups and downs. We often don't know the best choices to make, and our Angel is here to guide us to make the best choices for us. Communicating with your Angel is a similar process as communicating with your Higher self and Spirit/God.

4. The fourth and final step is to trust your Angel and trust yourself. The relationship that you establish with your Guardian angel is a magical bond and will change your life. You will begin to feel a sense of comfort, a peaceful knowing that you are never alone. It is not a good idea to ask your Angel for the lottery numbers as there are boundaries and ethics that the universe enforces. I do however recommend asking for the best choices in your business and your personal life. The more you work with your Angel, the quicker you will establish a relationship and trust the information that you are receiving.

My own Guardian Angel has helped many people who have come to me for assistance and questions. People are often shocked at the information my Angel provides to them. My Angel is always spot on. It often shocks me when I tell the person what she said, and whoever is receiving the message is comforted by her words of love and hope. I must be clear that the information that comes in is from my Guardian Angels and Spirit/God, I am just the vessel through which the messages are received. Fair warning, remember the information is coming to you from a Holy Angel not you. Yes, your intuition comes into play, but this is divine messaging coming through you and should be treated with reverence. If you ask to being in messages for other people from your Angel that's great just follow the steps. The Angels are very hard at work on earth right now helping us to establish a higher state of consciousness. Most of humanity has become materialistic and full of their own ego and have forgotten the ancient ways. The Angels are here to guide our soul's evolution to a spiritual awareness rather than a material need. This awakening is an important thing for us all to accomplish in this lifetime. My research along with my guided intuition has led me to believe that we are on this planet to evolve our souls. Spirit/God is not interested in how much money or things we accumulate while we are here or how great our physical appearance is. What truly matters is if you have developed your inner self, your soul. Have you been kind to others and forgiving of their mistakes? How many people have you helped along your journey? I believe the Angels are reminding us to have compassion for each other as the lessons here are not always easy. However, life was not meant to be difficult for any of us. It is meant to be enjoyed. The Angels rejoice when we laugh and when we dance and sing. They dance and sing with us. Laughter is honestly the best medicine for life! We each have a choice to listen to everybody else or do what feels right for you and yours. You can never go wrong when you are following your heart. Know that Spirit/God and the Holy Angels are here for you and love all of humanity. I believe they are rooting for us! Now that you have established a relationship with Spirit/God, the Goddess and your Guardian Angel expect miracles to occur in your life. We are energetic souls having a human experience. By connecting to Spirit/God and the Angels, along with the understanding of how the universe operates, your life will be forever changed for the better.

Section Six

The Spiritual Laws

Here are the spiritual Laws that are important for you to understand and reflect upon when you are making your way on your path in life. I have written the spiritual laws that I feel will inspire and assist the most people at this time.

These are simple principles to live by yet profound in many ways. I feel blessed to have the opportunity to share this wisdom with you now. As you begin practicing this new insight, please share your wisdom with others, and lead by example. This will truly help uplift humanity and change the world with your light!

Change is essential for the continuation of humanity. These Spiritual Laws are universal and important for all people to know about, to understand and to successfully live by. This wisdom within these principles is a way of living to bring about joy, fulfillment, and love to humanity. A change in society.

Learning the truth is how we elevate our souls and live a joyful, prosperous, and fulfilling life.

And as this wisdom is passed down to our children and grandchildren, the new generations will thrive!

Spiritual Law reminds us to honor our parents as this is who you chose to learn the most from in this lifetime. You don't have to like them or agree with their parenting skills but love them for who they are, as they are the souls who brought you into being. Honor all the children as we are the watchers of the children. We are here to protect them and teach them good and moral ways to live and prosper. So that future generations thrive!

Know that you are connected to everyone and everything as we are all energetic souls who are connected. Send out the love energy vibration and you will attract more love into your life!

The Universal Laws are in place to maintain balance. An energetic balance of our souls while in these bodies. Here are the laws.

The First Spiritual Law
Be True to Yourself

"To Thine Own Self Be True"
William Shakespeare

You are a beautiful soul, Be you!

Do not be afraid to be who you truly are and to say what you stand for! Your true essence is held in your heart and your soul.

Trust yourself, your intuition, that feeling inside of your heart and soul. Learning to trust yourself is not an easy feat. Your confidence will automatically grow as you do begin to get in touch with your inner self.

You will reach that point when you know you have made the best choices for yourself not caring about what others may think of you or how they will react to your choices. It's peaceful knowing that you are on your path. Many people refer to this behavior as being your authentic self, living your best life. I believe we should all be who we are, we are all beautiful souls.

According to Spiritual Law you may have anything your heart desires.

Let's begin by addressing frequency and universal energy.

"Everything is energy and that's all here is to it" Einstein also said, *"Energy cannot be created or destroyed, it can only be changed from one form to another."*
E=mc2 the theory of relativity, it says that matter and energy are interchangeable.
Albert Einstein

Humanity is at a point where most people understand that everything is made up of energy, and that this energy originated from the Divine Source that created all. The Creator of the rocks, trees, plants, the birds, and bees, the fish in the sea all are living energies. They are all as alive and vibrant as we are. Humanity is now recognizing that everything is alive and full of universal energy. We as humans are waking up to our unique gifts that make each of us unique energetic beings.

The vibrations of our thoughts, words, and emotions go out into the universe and your frequency is received. This is how the universe is set up. The answer you are searching for may not be what you imagined it would be. Often, we receive something even better than we had anticipated receiving. Know that what you ask for or prayed for may not come in your time frame, but you are heard and answered by the Divine Source, God. And your answer will come in divine timing.

Now that you know everything is energy and frequency you understand the power of the spoken word, the power of your thoughts and emotions. Prayer is the perfect example. When a group prays in unison with the same intention, the results are amazingly powerful, and miracles occur.

Truth be told, when we allow outside influences to affect us it can become a chain that binds us to a lower frequency, and we become stuck in this frequency of trying to please others. This occurs when we are concerned about others' opinions of who we are and who others believe we should be. Detach yourself, be true to yourself. When we release attachments to what others think of us, their judgments of us, we go free!

When we release what no longer serves us, then we cannot be manipulated emotionally. This is when you are in your own power. This is how you free your soul to become your true authentic self.

Our souls know who we are and can feel the freedom when we are in our own power.

Stand strong in knowing you are a child of the Divine Source and are protected by your Guardian Angel when you believe. Believe in yourself as we all have the knowledge inside of ourselves, we just must wake up that wisdom that lies deep within our souls.

Regardless of your religion, you can have faith in a higher power, an energy that loves humanity unconditionally. The love you receive will fill that empty space.

We are all connected regardless of our color or nationality we are all the same. We are all energetic souls of light and are all worthy of love.

It may seem surprising to many of you, but we all have come here by choice. To be here at this time of awakening. It is the most exciting time in history to be alive, to witness the prophecies come to pass. Mankind is learning a huge lesson. Each of us must look for the truth within and have compassion and love for each other.

We are all here to learn life lessons, lessons you can only learn while in a physical body through the five senses. This is not news to many; most people today realize that we are here to grow at a soul level. Every situation in our lives creates a learning experience to bring about a better understanding of life and enhances our wisdom and true essence.

These life lessons evolve your souls to new heights. The roadblocks that we encounter along the way is what will create soul growth and what creates who you are and who you will become.

As you progress through life and learn what you came here to tackle, you become your authentic self. Some of us choose not to progress and that's each soul's choice. Many people are waking up and realizing that they have been born at this time to experience and help humanity raise our vibration to love, kindness and compassion for all of humanity and for the plants, trees and animals that live here with us on the earth.

We are all connected yet each of us has our own unique gift that makes us special. Not one of us is exactly alike. It's your uniqueness that is your true essence. As we all begin to explore ourselves in this Age of Aquarius, we become more aware of our gifts.

When you go with the flow and be who you truly are, you are more in tune with the universe, the energetic powers that be. Life will flow more smoothly for you as you connect to this high vibration of source.

Our universe is set up in such a way that we receive exactly what we feel we are worth and exactly what we ask for. Choose your words carefully when you are asking, be specific as we receive to exactly what we request. Please remember you are creating your reality as we are all manifesting our own lives right now.

We as humans can manifest, to create what we would like. If you are new to this concept, please try to remain open minded.

When you ask for something, the key is to know in your heart and soul that you will receive it or something better. The universe has its own timing, so I want to mention this now. We can manifest anything into our reality, some things quicker than others. But remember the timing that you will receive your wish, or something even better comes in divine timing not your own. We are not in charge. Yes, we have free will to choose and to manifest but our creator, Source Energy, the Divine Source/ God knows better than we do, like a parent who knows when to give their child a cookie or a potato chip and know they will not choke. The universal powers-that-be would like to grant us our wish. People ask me all the time if they can manifest for someone else.

You can send good vibrations to another person, good wishes, and prayers, but the most powerful energy to send to heal anyone is to send them love. The energy of love is the most powerful energy in the universe.

I have learned that we must balance our energy between the earth and the spiritual part of our lives to achieve a balance. Many of you have heard this term and many of you ground yourself daily.

To achieve a state of balance we need to be grounded energetically. Grounding is connecting to the earth's energies. Before we wore shoes, we were all much more grounded. The energy of the earth is extremely healing to the body. "I see nature as healing because of the conductive support the earth provides the human body," says Laura Koniver, MD, author of *The Earth Prescription.*

"The earth pulses out an electromagnetic frequency – known as the Schumann Resonance – and the human body is fully conductive. Every single cell in our entire body becomes immediately grounded whenever we physically touch the earth directly. Twenty years of medical studies on grounding show that when we are connected to the earth's energy, our bodies naturally go into a healing state.

There are certain healing energies within the earth that are natural and our bodies need and thrive from. We need these energies to be healthy and vibrant.

Many of us grew up in the country and ran around barefoot all summer long, I know I did and was grounding without even knowing it. The truth is we become busy working and living our lives and may not go out into nature very often if at all. The good news is we can ground from anywhere even if you're living on concrete and pavement. If you have a grassy area or a park you can go to and just be with the plants and the trees, do it and take off your shoes!

My patio is concrete and then gravel, so I visualize roots coming out of my feet and my tailbone rooting into the earth every day. Some days my feet have white flowers coming out the top and other days just the green stems and roots growing down into the earth to root me in for the day.

It is up to you and your imagination. Visualization is extremely powerful it is the energy of your intention that creates the grounding energy into the earth. When I do not ground, I am not my balanced self and am out of my body. Grounding brings you back into your body and helps to balance your energy fields.

A Canadian researcher by the name of Francis Nixon was a pioneer in the study of Vivaxis, the spiral of life. He said that the Vivaxis is your life axis, your energy umbilical cord to the planet.

It is where you plug into the earth. This is the connection to the earth energies. Vivaxis in Latin means life and center. He demonstrated that the earth energy healing frequency from our planet's core is connected to an individual's own energetic field.

As recently as 2019 biologists and neuroscientists at Caltech and the University of Tokyo studied and concluded that humans have a geomagnetic sense, just as honeybees respond behaviorally to it. The energetic vibration of truth is picked up by the powers that be just as the flowers energetically feel the change of the season and a bird's song. The bird's vibration helps the flowers grow. When you have grateful energy, the earth picks up on the frequency as it is a live living entity.

The Second Spiritual Law
Be Truthful and Honest

Honesty is the first chapter in the book of wisdom.
Thomas Jefferson

The Golden Rule says, "Do unto others as you would have them do unto you.". You don't want anyone to lie to you or deceive you in friendship, love or in business.

This means that you cannot tell a lie to anyone, not even a wee lie. When you hear the saying,

"The truth will set you free," it is correct. You don't want to carry around the bad energy created by fibbing, it will weigh you down energetically. Our vibration is so important to our health and wellbeing and to keep it high we must be truthful to ourselves and to others. Lying is a lower vibrational habit; possibly the result of feeling fearful or an insecurity, or possibly learned behavior, hereditary; regardless of its origin it's a nasty habit.

The universe has your back when you are connected energetically, to Spirit/God, because of this connection when you do the right thing, you are rewarded by the universal energies. The universe and Spirit/God pick up on our energy and give us back exactly what energy we put out to the world with our words, thoughts, and emotions. When we speak negatively about another person that spoken vibration comes back to its source; you are given back what you gave out.

The same is true for example if someone lies to you or tries to deceive you or betrays your trust;

please know that the universe is taking care of their deception on your behalf. This is how universal energy works. You don't have to get even with the liar, the energy created by the lie will come back to them tenfold.

Protecting one's energy field is extremely important. Have you ever felt uncomfortable when someone you don't know gets too close to your personal space? They are affecting your energy field, and your field does not recognize this person's energy and the body responds with a fight or flight response. This is exactly why it is imperative for everyone to set clear boundaries in their life and honor their own space.

Boundaries are a necessity for all of us to have. Set boundaries for yourself. It is important not to let other people, even if it's family, a friend, or your boss invade your sacred space. You must draw the line for your own healthy energetics.

Your space and energetic field must remain clear for your vibration to stay high in a joyful state of peace and balance.

When we honor ourselves as well as other people, honorable and truthful energy flows out into the universe and is returned to us tenfold.

Setting clear boundaries with people is key. Respect for yourself and your time must be your highest priority, along with respect for your fellow man. Do not let other people bring you down to a lower level energetically.

Protect your energy field and you are protecting your overall health as they are connected. Don't let energy vampires drain you of your good energy as this will bring down your immune system.

People who do not have their own light, full of uplifting energy and love will try to drain you of yours to fill their void. Many times, people have a low opinion of themselves and may portray this type of behavior. They are searching for the light outside of themselves as they are unable to bring their own light in. People who have high vibrations are often targets for low vibrational beings searching for love and joy outside of themselves. It is important that we recognize that this does occur. I have witnessed a spouse of low vibration living off their partner's light energy.

The person with the light energy can produce more but after a long period of time becomes draining and the other person does not grow energetically on their own.

It is important to be truthful in life, to be honest. It is always best to be honest with others and to be honest with yourself. You don't want to cheat yourself, do you?

As a gifted person with claircognizance I clearly know if someone is lying to me. And I want to tell you it is often difficult to know that someone you love is lying to you. Betrayal and deceit from another person are difficult emotions to overcome.

The truth is often heartbreaking and difficult to bear. But knowing that the truth will set you free!

"And you will know the truth, and the truth will set you free."
John 8:32
NIV Study Bible

Often, we want to see the best in people and overlook their flaws, it's human nature. Although it's always surprising to me when people are deceptive and untruthful with their actions and with their words. Life has taught me that actions always speak louder than someone's words.

We cannot be disappointed when people aren't truthful to us, as everybody's journey is not the same. We are all here to learn and sometimes we must let go and not take their lies personally.

There are always reasons why things happen the way they do; maybe there is a lesson for that person to gain in the process.

We don't always know the reasoning behind events. There may be a hidden treasure in the lesson they are learning.

If you are looking for the truth pay attention to a person's actions, their behavior. This will tell you all you need to know. Use your intuition and ask your Angel for confirmation.

To overcome the betrayal of a person may take years to heal from. The wounds are often deep leaving scars to heal. This is where forgiveness comes in. It's important to forgive others if you want to be forgiven. Please know that all life experiences promote growth.

"Freedom is the open window through which pours the sunlight of the human spirit and of human dignity."
Herbert Hoover

Freedom is the right to live the way that you choose to. This means the freedom to go where you choose, buy what you like, eat your favorite foods, live where you desire and have the life you choose. Freedom gives us choice.

The freedom to choose our own path in life. Some of us are fortunate to be free to choose our college, career, partner, and home while others do not have those luxuries. Regardless of your situation or your station in life, we all can choose the path of love and light, kindness, and forgiveness to guide us along the way. A path filled with truth honesty and compassion for us and for our fellow man.

As you understand the life lessons that your soul came here to learn, you are naturally elevated to a higher frequency and will see positive changes in your life.

The Third Spiritual Law
Forgive, Let It Go!

"Forgive all who have offended you, not for them, but for yourself."
Harriet Nelson

The most important truth I can disclose to you about forgiveness is; when you forgive others you free yourself! I must be honest and say that forgiveness is not an easy thing to do.

True forgiveness is feeling the forgiveness in your heart and in your soul. Letting go of the hurt,

anger, resentment whatever the feeling is and releasing that energy out into the universe. Send it to the light!

Often people hold a grudge and would like to seek revenge of some sort when they have been treated unfairly. I am sure you can relate to the vengeful emotions that can arise when a disagreement or offensive words or gestures are said. But you don't have to be vengeful, and retaliate in any war, the universe takes care of this on your behalf.

The way the universe handles revenge is in a patient manner; slowly sneaking up on the avenger when they least expect it. This is another reason it is good to forgive and let go, know that the universe has your back. This is the way Spirit/ God, the Divine Source set it up. It's amazing when you think about it. Now you know how the divine one keeps tabs on us all. It's all energetically connected. It's like Santa Claus knowing if you're naughty or nice. Of course, Spirit/God knows your heart and your energy field and can energetically tap into your unique frequency. God, the Divine Source knows your heart, and that spark of creative energy within and this is how the Creator of the universe knows what's going on with you, all the divine needs to do is to connect with your unique vibration.

Please release all resentment, anger, frustration, hatefulness of another person's words or their actions. Holding onto to negative energy lowers your vibration which in turn brings you down to that person's level that you are so angry with. For your own wellbeing, now is the time to release all emotions that you have been holding onto as we are elevating to higher frequency which brings love and joy in your life.

Many of us hold onto unkind words spoken to us or the hold onto that hurt we have experienced through sheer unkindness, lies betrayal and deceit. It is imperative that you know that the person who said those terrible things or acted foolishly or unkind are hurting inside of themselves.

These are souls who do not know how to find love in their own hearts and soul and so they hurt others hoping they can feel better about themselves. It's as simple as understanding that misery loves company. The mindset is that these folks don't want you to be happy, joyful, and prosperous when they are not.

When we do not forgive each other, it does bring disease into the body. When we have health issues the culprit is the cause of our energy fields being out of balance.

When we experience loss, anger, deception, betrayal, trauma of any kind our bodies are affected energetically. We are energetic souls inside of these wonderful bodies, but we have not realized the energetic connection to our emotions. Not forgiving and holding onto those emotions is one of the main reasons for health issues. I can attest to this fact myself.

When I was going through a divorce my thyroid became a huge problem. It took many months to come to a place of forgiveness and feeling the emotions and releasing them to come back into balance. I also found myself going back to the doctor several times to adjust my medication before my thyroid gland settled down. I use this as an example as we all have things happen to us in life and must release the trauma to heal. Our body tells us what is going on with us emotionally. It is signaling us to pay attention!

This story is a brief example of letting go of the past.

A Buddhist Story.
This is how the story was told to me.

One evening two monks were returning to the monastery where they lived. It had been a rainy day and as they traveled there were many puddles of water alongside the road where they were walking. At one place they both saw a beautiful young woman standing by the roadside. She was unable to move ahead because a puddle of water was in her way. The older of the two monks approached her and lifted her into his arms and gently carried her across the mud puddles to the other side of the road. When the two monks reached their destination the younger monk said, "as monks we cannot touch a woman, so why did you lift that woman on the roadside?"

The older monk answered yes, my brother. The younger monk seemed confused and asked the older monk, "how is it you lifted that woman on the roadside?" The elder monk smiled at his brother and replied, "I left her on the other side of the road, but you are still carrying Her?"

Many people carry the burdens from their past with them their entire lives. This is often a result of a past trauma that has not been released. These are memories that remain alive in our bodies if we keep them alive by reliving them again. You see our thoughts are energetic and affect us physically.

Our thoughts have such power over our bodies, that the body believes that we are living the same scenario over again energetically. We as humans are very powerful beings and have not been told or shown our gifts.

When we think about past experiences the negative energy of these events weighs us down emotionally and energetically. Many of us were taught to hold onto the anger and resentment of events at a young age and have carried this pattern with us through to adulthood.

Free yourself and forgive, let it go. You will feel much better, as if a weight has been lifted off your shoulders. I experienced my mother's anger as a child and carried it with me for most of my life until I released the energy of the emotion, I had taken on her anger without realizing it but have now released it.

Often, we must distance ourselves from people who we love but no longer serve our best interests. These are the friends, coworkers or relatives that do not bring us joy, only sorrow. This is when you walk away and save yourself!

There is a huge divide right now in the world. The differences between people and their views and beliefs have become clear. Many of the separations are politically motivated, but often it is our programming and belief system, how we perceive the world. The fact remains that many of us have had to walk away from friends and family members to remain balanced and sane. As you connect with a higher energetic vibration People you thought you would always stay close with are not at the same vibration as you any longer and you begin to recognize this. Remember, we all do not grow at the same rate so no judgments of others who are not there yet. Be the example for change.

We are living in a time where walking away from a job, a spouse or a family member is often necessary to keep your energy fields clear. Keep your distance from people's energy that does not serve you and your highest good.

Everyone is learning at a different pace so you may see things completely differently from your brother or friend. This is all about how you see the reality of life and how much you have worked on yourself to elevate your soul. When I say "worked on yourself" I am referring to going within and cleaning out your closet. Releasing emotions that you have held onto that no longer serve you!

We all have skeletons in our closets that have been hidden that we need to release the emotions of.

These emotions remain in our bodies unless they are dealt with; or released. These are emotions that do not serve us, but we have chosen not to experience the pain at the time or the fear, the hurt or the anger. To release the energy that caused that emotion you must feel the feeling and then let it go, release the anger, fear, frustration whatever the emotion is inside of you, let it go.

I have noticed that when people hit rock bottom and then climb their way back up the ladder

their eyes are wide open! They see the truth. The more we all work on ourselves on the inside the more we heal and elevate our vibration. We begin to see things in a new light. We begin to see life from an aerial view, a new perspective is born.

We are here to elevate our souls to a vibration of love, pure love for yourself and everything and everyone around you.

God, the Source created this universe with the energy of love. We are all learning to connect back to each other and back to the source that is, pure love.

People that you have known for a long time even grew up with and thought you would always stay close with you realize are not on the same vibration as you and you begin to recognize this.

Family members may not be where you are in this evolutionary process but do not judge them as we all evolve at our own time. This is one of the signs that you are seeing the truth as you recognize the patterns in others and come to an and understanding of why truth is so important.

"Don't judge each day by the harvest you reap but by the seeds that you plant."
Robert Louis Stevenson

The Fourth Spiritual Law
You Reap What You Sow

We reap the harvest of the seeds we plant in our lives. This is one of the most important laws of the universe. A law that should be taught when we are small children.

It's imperative that I address the energy of the spoken word, the written word, and your thoughts.

All have energy and all have the power to create your reality.

When we speak, we are creating, when we think we are creating, and when we feel we are creating our reality. What you think of yourself is who you become. What you think about all day is where you are headed. Pay attention to your thoughts as the energy flows where your attention goes.

We are such powerful creatures that don't even realize our full potential. We can have anything we desire or better through the power of our manifestations. We are spiritual beings with the power to create our reality. We are little creators because we are made in the image of Spirit/ God and have a spark of the divine in each of us, that Source energy, the light who created the entire universe.

So, if you don't like your story, create a new one. Each day is a new day to create whatever you choose. Only you can change your life as you are the artist of the painting, and this is your picture, stage play, your movie.

When you are planting your seeds speak what you desire into the universe. You can write down your desires in a journal. Journaling is freeing for the soul as you can get your thoughts out and onto paper. I write to God and to the Goddess daily. It's a way of communicating one's hopes and dreams.

The vibration of your words is the most powerful manifesting tool we have, whether by affirmation, prayer or speaking out loud to the Divine Source, speak about what you want to create. Act as if your seeds have already grown and cultivated. You must feel as if your vision, your manifestation, has already materialized. What does it feel like when you receive your wish?

Knowing what it feels like when your seeds have taken root and are fully grown is key to the process. What does your manifestation feel like? If you can get into that energy, your manifestation will arrive quicker.

Often people begin by visualizing their desire and imagining what it will feel like when the seeds that have been planted have grown. A big part of manifesting your dreams is to pretend you already have acquired what you are searching for. The universe picks up on your energy and sends it back to you in different forms and in various ways. When you believe it and can feel your manifestation the universe can too.

Our voice holds a frequency that is unique to each one of us. Our voice is the strongest

manifesting power tool we have! Our own voice is so powerful that when we speak, our unique vibration goes out to the universe, and we are answered. The universe knows exactly who we are. God knows all the children of the world and loves them all.

Now that you know you're planting seeds; what kind of seeds are you planting with your words?

What are you saying about yourself? What are you saying about others? It is the vibration of your voice that the universe picks up on and your physical vibration, your emotions that the universe feels to determine how to respond to you.

What type of seeds are you planting today? What are the intentions and words you are putting out bringing you back?

Energy Flows Where Your Attention Goes. The energy of your thoughts and words have power! Whatever you think about all day long and feel passionate about and speak about is what you are manifesting into your life right now!

All you must do is speak it into existence and visualize what you're attempting to manifest,

know you will receive it or something better and let it go. The universe is set up in such a way that you can manifest anything if you put enough energy into it.

Simple right? These are the principles of manifestation, but it is not always so easy to accomplish if you don't believe. Not always easy to do, it takes practice but that's ok, practice makes perfect manifestations.

Pay attention to what you are saying, the words you are speaking have vibration and meaning.

See if the words you are speaking fit your vision for your future. What are you creating with your words, thoughts, and feelings? Know that what you say while in this life matters. Your words and your thoughts have power!

Bad seeds bring in a bad harvest and the next harvest will be bad as well. This is why we plant good seeds in our children by teaching them kindness, love, and compassion for others.

Regardless of a person's color or nationality or their religious beliefs, we are all souls in these bodies growing to become connected loving humans.

Just as a farmer plants the seeds in the ground, we put our intentions out to the universe. We decide what we want and begin to manifest. We have a choice of what actions we take and what words we speak and what we teach our children and grandchildren by our example. What will you speak into manifestation today? What kind of seeds are you planting to harvest?

I know you may have heard the story of "The Little Red Hen." I told this story to my children when they were little many times as I wanted them to learn about pitching in and helping others.

This Famous fable teaches all of us that we reap what we sew.

The Little Red Hen

This is how the story was told to me.

The little Red Hen decided to make fresh wheat bread but knew it would be a lot of work. She asks if any one of her friends would like to have fresh bread? They all said," yes, that would be lovely." She told her friends that she was going to plant wheat seeds to grow the grain for the bread and asked if anyone wanted to help her? They all said, "no."

The little red hen moved forward and planted the seeds of wheat herself. She watered the plants, tended to them and she grew beautiful wheat. She then asked her friends, who will help me harvest the wheat? No one replied, so she harvested it herself. She asked her friends "who will help me make the wheat into flour?", but there were no takers. She made the flour herself. She then decided to make the bread. She asked her friends one last time, "who will help me make the bread?"

Sadly, her friends were lazy and did not want to pitch in and help her. The little Red Hen followed the recipe and mixed all the ingredients together and placed the loaves of bread in the oven to bake. She made the best wheat bread you ever tasted; you could smell the aroma of freshly baked bread as it came out of the oven throughout the entire neighborhood.

All her friends came to see what she was cooking, as it smelled so wonderful. The little Red Hen said, "it's the bread, they all wanted a taste, but she declined."

I planted the seeds myself; I harvested the wheat myself; I made the wheat into flour and now I have made the most delicious bread, and I am going to eat it all myself, and she did.

This story stands truer than ever today. Everybody wants a piece of the bread, but nobody wants to do the actual work to create it. Reaping what you sew is how we create our dreams and make them manifest. We cannot expect things to occur without thought and action. Spiritual law is in place to help us achieve our goals, but you must do the earthly work to make it happen.

Manifestation requires seeds from the spiritual world and some from the material world to make the magic happen. We plant the seeds, first in our mind, then often we apply our thoughts to paper. We speak about our dreams that we want to achieve and then we must take the steps to create our vision. We may daydream of our dream coming to fruition and that is perfect. If you can see it, then you can manifest it. There are many seeds that you can plant but only you know what kind of seeds you will plant. But remember you must do your part and do the work that is required.

Some requests of the universe will deliver very quickly to us but it's the big things, the most desired things that take the most time. The universe must orchestrate the big things Many of us, myself included are her learning patience waiting for the big dreams to manifest into reality. We are in a giant matrix creating and co-creating all the time. This web that we are designing affects everyone as we are all connected. The seeds your neighbor plants can affect you in some way.

Now you see that if we all planted seeds of love, kindness, joy, compassion, and friendship how the matrix would expand, and that vibration would change the world! This is what I hope that we will all plant good seeds that will grow and we can harvest the rewards and share that harvest with our friends.

Understand that many people on the planet are sewing bad seeds. And when they plant bad seeds, bad things grow! Know that you cannot change another person or prevent them from making the choices they do. This becomes a generational pattern unless someone breaks the cycle.

A good example is that you love your family and friends, but you cannot allow them to bring change to your high vibrational state of being. If they affect you emotionally that is affecting you energetically and in turn psychically.

You may have to weed out a few friends and family to stay healthy and in a high vibrational state of happiness. The love for yourself must be greater than the love of another. Love your body and your energy. Choose only joy! You can send love and prayers to those you care about and that love energy will make a difference every single time you send it ours. Remember whatever you think about; speak of and feel goes out into the universe and is returned to you. When you send out love and blessings to others that same energy is returned to you.

"The joy and fulfillment we are searching for is love. Love of the self and of God."
Nancy Yearout

The Fifth Spiritual Law
Let the Love Flow

Opening our hearts to receiving love and sending out the love vibration to others creates harmony and bliss. Sending the love vibration is the most healing and kind act a person can do for themselves and for the receiver. Love contains an enormous power that lies in the frequency we call love. Love is the vibration that created the universe that we live in today. Love is the vibration that heals everything, and love is absolutely the answer we are all searching for. Love is the ultimate healing miracle!

The Spiritual Law of unconditional love reveals that love is the healing miracle we all search for. The fulfillment we yearn for. Love fills our heart and our soul with the highest frequency there is and when this happens, miracles occur. The spiritual law is that when you send out love you receive the love back and often tenfold. The energy of love is powerful and will heal the body, mind, and spirit. I believe that what everyone on the planet is searching for is love.

Love is an emotion that is felt at different levels of intensity. The love of flowers; the love of skiing or playing a game are all expressions of love but different than the love of a child, a parent, or a spouse.

All are fabulous examples of love.

We express the emotion of love differently to different people, and to various things and activities. Regardless of your love for a person or the love of a thing, love is the number one feeling we are all searching for, crave and in many cases are willing to do anything to obtain.

When you're in love it is the most marvelous feeling in the universe! Being in love is indescribable. You can't wait to see that person or hear from them by phone. New love is grand, as sparks fly! But true love takes time. True love is taking the time and effort to get to know one another. Love is coming from a place of understanding, kindness and compassion in good times and in bad times. True love is the energetic connection you feel of another person's heart and soul. The appearance of a person is how they portray or present themselves to others and the outside world; yet the inside is where the true essence of love resides. An open heart is revealing your true self and loving unconditionally, without rules or expectations. I do agree you must be best friends and be attracted to that person sexually for it to work. These are the two key ingredients to a successful relationship. And most importantly, learn to laugh a lot with each other, have fun! Take life lightly as the Angels do.

Many people believe that love will come into their lives by accumulating material things or obtaining financial gain, social status, or the trophy partner! Simply said, "That is not love." Love is the connection to another's soul in such a way that you feel energetically as one.

As we evolve to kinder souls, I believe the act of making love will deepen emotionally between two people. True love is a sacred bond between two people's hearts as it is often said that two hearts beat as one. Love is the healing gift for all of humanity to open.

Everyone is looking for love. But everyone is looking for love in all the wrong places. The love people are searching for is within each one of us. It is not outside of us. There is a disconnect in our society when it comes to love as people who grow up with the idea that love, and joy are outside of themselves. It seems many of us are searching for love but can't seem to find it. The need to be loved, to feel love and to give love to another living being is natural. What we have not been taught in our society is to love ourselves and Spirit/God, the Divine Source Energy.

The love we are searching for is the treasure that lies within. The love of the self is the greatest love of all, as we all contain a spark of Spirit/God that Divine Source within our soul. When you are connected and truly love yourself then you can truly love another person. The treasure lies within you. The love we are searching for is already inside of us with that spark from Spirit/ God, the Divine Source. We must tap into our soul to find it.

We are ascending to a higher frequency, and that frequency is love and it begins with each one of us. Once we are full of love in our own heart, we radiate that love vibration out into the universe.

With love in your heart, you are spreading your light to your family, friends and neighbors and strangers. You become the love and light that is so needed in this world to raise the vibration to kindness, compassion, and forgiveness. Love is such a strong emotion and can solve all our disagreements with its energy. Love brings us understanding and opens the awareness to hear another person's point of view.

AuraHealth.com says that love has scientifically proven to carry a unique frequency, which is 528 HZ and is also known as the frequency of Love, some call it the *"Miracle Tone"*,

Love is the cure for everything that ails us (our energy fields) as there is confirmation that the frequency of love has been used by healers in advanced civilizations to create miracles!

Ancient priests say that the energy of love has the power to reduce anxiety and stress in our lives.

Love is the strongest vibration in the universe and heals everything.

The frequency of love releases emotional blockages that may cause disease in the body.

The vibration of musical tones will assist in healing your chakras and your aura, your energy field.

Many energy healers use crystal singing bowls to bring about the healing vibration needed to bring about balance in the body. Music soothes the heart and soul when it comes to matters of the heart.

I believe all people are searching for love. Many who have grown up not knowing what true love really is and are seeking to find the magic for their hearts to be fulfilled.

When you are in a new relationship, how do you know if it's real love? The energy of love is what we all crave but there are a lot of narcissists out in the world too. So be careful who you choose to share your energy with. Pay attention to your intuition, you know the feeling when someone honestly cares about you, not the outside but the inner you.

Here is a fabulous quote that talks about real love of another.

"I love you not because of who you are, but because of who I am when I am with you."
Roy Croft

The most powerful and fulfilling love is the love of Spirit/God, the Divine Source Energy. Experiencing a connection with God is not only enlightening but fulfilling. There is no greater love than that of the almighty who is the energy of light and love itself. Connecting to the Source Energy is life changing in so many ways. The light energy you receive when you connect is healing to your body and your soul.

There is so much love that is given out and received freely each day by this Holy light. When sent out the love vibration returns to you and often tenfold. The energy of love is powerful it can heal the body, mind, and spirit which is changing our world.

There are many emotions and feelings related to the energy of love. For example, there is the love of a child by its mother, the love of a mother and a father by their child, a grandmother and grandfather's love for their grandchildren, an aunt's love for a niece or nephew, a sister or a brother's love for each other, or the love you hold for your cousin or your uncle. All have different love vibrations attached to them, but the commonality remains the frequency of love is felt within us. The vibration of love is everywhere.

No one person or thing can create our joy, love, and happiness. If we believe that someone or something brings us our joy, we lose our own zest for life. When we give our power away to a person place or thing, we lose ourselves. Be aware of how important it is to remain in your own power, to be true to yourself and to your heart and soul.

We cannot rely on someone or something in our lives to make us feel happy and fulfilled. We can however depend on good loyal friends and amazing love relationships to bring joy to our lives and allow us the space to be who we are and allow the space needed to fulfill our purpose in this life.

This quote is a nice reminder of how friendships turn into love relationships.

"Love is a friendship that has caught fire!"
Ann Landers

Most of us grew up with the idea that love, and joy are outside of ourselves to search for love from other people. I searched for a long time until I realized that the love, I was looking for was the love of the divine which was in myself. No one ever mentions while growing up that you are supposed to love yourself. Today many cultures are talking about the importance of loving who you are and how wonderful to see this change occurring.

No one person or thing can create joy, love and happiness for a person. We create our own reality every day and choose how we are going to show up in the world. You can show up with love in the heart for all you will encounter each day or address life with anger and fear. Each one of us has a choice to make every single day when we wake up.

Often our struggles in life propel us to search for answers to life's questions to give us a new understanding of life and the meaning of love. When we search for the answers, we go within; and within all of us is a soul that yearns to be fulfilled, to feel joyful and loved. Most of us search outside of ourselves and try to fill the void with the material items of the world but that never suffices.

To remain in your own power to be true to yourself and to your heart and soul you must love yourself first. We create what we believe.

If we believe that someone or something is needed to bring us our joy in our lives, it's a sign to go within ourselves. When we give our power away to a person place or thing, we lose ourselves.

We cannot depend on someone else or something in our lives to make us feel happy and fulfilled. This is how our society has evolved. I am not sure how we lost our love of self, along the way but many souls have. I am here to say you can get it back! Break the pattern.

Start connecting with the earth's energy, the high vibrations of source and the Angels who are our helpers.

The light and love vibration that you receive from the Spirit/ God, will bring a smile onto your face, and fill your heart with joy. The divine unconditional love will bring a peace and balance to your life.

So many of us are searching for love on the outside of ourselves. Many people look for love as they accumulate material things or obtain financial gain. The love of money, social status, or the trophy partner! Simply said, "that is not what love is."

You cannot buy love with money or power. Love is a natural emotion that occurs when two people are on the same wavelength are at the same vibration. Now that you understand energy you can see how two people attract each other energetically. Many break-ups occur when one of the two grows and the other person doesn't. Leaving an energetic imbalance. There are many young people today who think sex is love. Making love with a person is meant to be an intimate encounter between two people who feel deeply about each other. The act itself has been exploited since the beginning of time.

When we attempt to manipulate a person or a situation to have love it's a quick path to a failed relationship. When a new love relationship begins everything is always great at first wine and roses, but the newness eventually wears off and it's the substance of true love and friendship, honesty, and compassion and of course kindness that is the glue to keep you together. If there is no substance, there is no relationship.

It's all about the treasure that lies within our hearts that is where true love resides.

Many people feel that if they have another person who loves them, they will be fulfilled but again, these relationships are short-lived. They are out of balance. The best relationships are two people who are equally met with love for the inside of the person not the outside, not their looks. Looks are great but the beauty and the treasure lie within.

Love is a sacred bond between a person, or a can be a thing as everything is energy. You can have a love bond between yourself and your garden for example, your apple tree, or your roses. But the idea is to find the love within yourself. The universe picks up on our unique vibration, so it is important that you love yourself to bring in that love energy to yourself.

There is plenty of love out there to connect with but learn to love yourself first and you will attract the person who is on your same vibration as yourself.

I can attest that I searched for love as many people do for a long time after growing up with a narcissistic mother and a workaholic father. I kept looking for love and it wasn't until I became still and began to connect with, Spirit/God Energy and the love energy; is when I realized I was not alone. What I had been searching was the energy of love from God. Now this love energy fills up my vessel every day with light when I connect.

After this miraculous event I began to find the love for myself that I had never paid much attention to. Many of us give of ourselves and neglect our own joy and fulfillment and love for the self which I have learned is not selfish at all.

Numerous songs have been written about love; poetry has been written throughout time. Amazing love stories have been written and portrayed by actors in movies and on television and in stage plays, showing the emotions and power of love and heart break.

There are many people who quote I Corinthians 13:4–8
From the Holy Bible NIV Version

Chapter 1

If I speak in the tongues[a] of men or of angels, but do not have love, I am only a resounding gong or a clanging cymbal.² If I have the gift of prophecy and can fathom all mysteries and all knowledge, and if I have a faith that can move mountains, but do not have love, I am nothing.³ If I give all I possess to the poor and give over my body to hardship that I may boast,[b] but do not have love, I gain nothing.⁴ Love is patient, love is kind. It does not envy, it does not boast, it is not proud.⁵ It does not dishonor others, it is not self-seeking, it is not easily angered, it keeps no record of wrongs.⁶ Love does not delight in evil but rejoices with the truth.⁷ It always protects, always trusts, always hopes, always perseveres.⁸

Love never fails. But where there are prophecies, they will cease; where there are tongues, they will be stilled; where there is knowledge, it will pass away.⁹ For we know in part, and we prophesy in part,¹⁰ but when completeness comes, what is in part disappears.¹¹ When I was a child, I talked like a child, I thought like a child, I reasoned like a child. When I became a man, I put the ways of childhood behind me.¹² For now we see only a reflection as in a mirror; then we shall see face to face. Now I know in part; then I shall know fully, even as I am fully known.¹³ And now these three remain: faith, hope and love. But the greatest of these is love.

The following is from my family Bible printed in the mid–late 1700's. I have included the first three verses of I Corinthians Chapter 13 to this interpretation of the scripture as it speaks of Charity.

I CORINTHIANS
CHAP. XIII 1–13

1. *Though I speak with the tongues of men and of angels, and have not charity, I am become as sounding brass or a tinkling cymbal.*

2. *And though I have the gift of prophecy and understand all mysteries, and all knowledge; and though I have all faith, so that I could remove mountains, and have not charity, I am nothing.*

3. *And though I bestow my goods to feed the poor, and though I give my body to be burned, and have not charity, it profiteth me nothing.*

4. *Charity suffereth long, and kind; charity envieth not; charity vaunteth not itself, is not puffed up,*

5. *Doth not behave itself unseemly, seeketh not her own, is not easily provoked, thinketh no evil.*

6. *Rejoice not in iniquity, but rejoiceth in the truth.*

7. *Beareth all things, believeth all things, hopeth all things, endureth all things.*

8. *Charity never faileth: Whether there be prophecies, they shall fail; whether there be tongues, they shall cease; whether there be knowledge, it shall vanish away.*

9. *For all we know in part, and we prophesy in part.*

10. *But when that which is perfect is come, then that which is perfect is come, then that which is in part shall be done away.*

11. *When I was a child, I spoke as a child, I understood as a child, I thought as a child; but when I became a man, I put away childish things.*

12. *For now we see through a glass; darkly; but then face to face: now I know in part; but then shall I know even as also I am known.*
13. *And now abideth faith, hope, charity, these three; but the greatest of these is charity.*

Charity is what is spoken of in these verses. How charity changed to love I am not sure, but the original Bible is stressing the importance of charity, of giving to those less fortunate than ourselves.

Many people contribute to charitable organizations and many people give of their time to help those less fortunate than themselves.

Charity is something that many of us have forgotten about. We get busy in our lives and striving to make it in our career and are busy taking care of the family that we often forget about the needy.

The definition for Charity from Webster's New World Dictionary:

Charity; love for one's fellow human beings; generosity toward the needy.

We must change how we view the world and others. Society has become so involved with the material world, cars, trucks, jeeps, designer clothes, purses and perfume, hair nail, clothes, and shoes. Our society has created a people who want to have it all. But when you acquire all the stuff are you truly happy?

The needy are just looking for a warm coat, decent clothing to wear, clean underwear, socks, and a good pair of shoes. There is such a great divide in wealth in the U.S. and abroad. It seems there are more homeless people than ever have been on this planet. Changing our society to be more charitable not just sending money but doing community service and helping your neighbors is what is going to make the change needed in the world.

"No man is as wise as Mother Earth."
Anasazi Foundation

The Sixth Spiritual Law
Take Care of and Honor Mother Earth

We Must Honor Mother Earth as the earth is where we reside.

This is our home, the place where we live and breathe. The earth provides us with our food to nourish our bodies and water to quench our thirst, the air to fill our lungs and breathe freely and fire to warm ourselves. The earth provides so that we may not only survive and live as healthy energetic people but thrive if we choose to.

Mother earth is also energetic, she is a living, breathing, and feeling entity we call planet earth. She is as alive as you and me. She reminds us of the feminine aspect of life. the Goddess has come back into our lives as many are discovering. The Goddess, the feminine energies that are emerging in our world are needed. The male and female energies are coming back into balance. The world has been dominated by the masculine energies for a long time and as the feminine energies resurface many changes will occur. The feminine will again be respected as it should have been all along as the co-creator of our world. The respect is and will return as we raise our vibration to a higher frequency of understanding.

Currently, the loss of respect for our planet has brought about earthquakes, hurricanes, tsunamis, volcano eruptions and major shifts within the earth's crust as she expresses her disappointment in mankind.

There are many who mine her resources, her minerals, and ores destroying whatever is in their path to obtain their treasures. The reality is that money is not important; as you can have all the money in the world and without food, water, air and fire the money is useless. Without the earth we could not survive.

We are provided for so well. Often, I am amazed that we can go to the store and buy anything we want. We are living in a time of much prosperity as anything we ask for can be delivered the same day or picked up at our convenience.

Think of how many options we have when it comes to food. We can go to the store and buy anything we desire. And the best thing is we can shop at any time day if we choose or have our food delivered to our door.

There are many different grocery stores to choose from as well as specialty meat stores; bakery's; coffee shops and tea shops, delicatessens, the list goes on.

We the people here in the United States and many countries abroad have numerous options when it comes to the choice of goods acquired that I am amazed that people get in and out of the store as quickly as they do. If you desire a salad just pick out your favorite lettuce regular or organic lettuce, romaine lettuce or butter leaf; heirloom; fresh green leaf lettuce green or Boston head lettuce. This is just the tip of the iceberg!

We have hundreds if not thousands of choices when we go to the grocery store to buy food. The number of food items that are available to us to purchase and consume is amazing. The potato chip aisle alone is overwhelming with wavey chips; oven roasted, crispy; twice baked; cheese puffs; tortilla chips and if it were not for mother earth there would be no corn chips. No corn chips at all.!

Think of how many restaurants there are on the planet and the variety of excellent cuisine available to us. We should be thanking mother earth daily for our food supply!

The earth provides grains of numerous varieties throughout the world. People grow rice, corn, soybeans, wheat, alfalfa just to name a few. The grains feed not only people but animals across the world.

When it comes to drinking and staying hydrated many people do prefer water. A twist of lemon or cucumber in your water can make the most refreshing drink ever! Mother earth provides water for all of us to drink. We quench our thirst with water, and we wash our clothes and cleanse ourselves with this precious liquid.

The earth's oceans and her seas hold numerous delicacies such as caviar and lobster tail, seaweed, and numerous species of fish. The air allows us to breathe and fire gives us the ability to warm ourselves and cook our food.

The earth provides everything we require to not only survive but to thrive here on the planet. Humanity is at a tipping point and if we want to continue to eat well; drink fresh water and breathe clean air we must do our part to pitch in and take care of mother earth. What we put into our body determines our health. And what we put into mother earth we get back as well.

It's the little things that make a difference such as picking up trash, recycling, growing your own vegetables and fruits, planting trees and growing plants not dumping toxic substances disposing of oil and toxins properly. Replacing what we take and replenishing the food supply for the next generation to come is huge. We need to concentrate on increasing our fresh vegetable and fruit supply and lessen our dependence on meat. The meat industry must keep up with the demand and in doing so does not always produce the ideal end products. I feel a little bit of meat is good but like everything, eat meat in moderation. Our diets lack in fresh fruits and vegetables when there are so many choices for us in these food groups. Nuts of all kinds are also a huge benefit to the body; the nutritional factors are so much better than fast food for a snack. We need to change it up and make fresh food the most popular thing to eat and watch humanity thrive.

Our oceans have sadly been polluted to the point that we have to gather the plastics and trash that has been tossed into the ocean and get it out! We are poisoning the water and the all the living creatures within it. I feel that plastic has been the largest contributor to polluting our earth and killing our animals. I know you have seen many different animals that have gotten their head stuck in a plastic container or dolphins tangled up in plastic netting. It does not decompose. There is a need to find a better way to handle the recycling of plastics.

Spiritual law says to honor the earth where we live; breathe and thrive. Spending as much time as you can in nature as the plants and trees is calming as their vibration is healing. They have fabulous earth vibrations and will assist in balancing your energy fields by being in contact with them. Flowers, plants of all kinds and trees generate healing vibrations to balance your energy fields and uplift your soul.

Experience the beauty of nature, it will rejuvenate your soul. The life force energy that is emitted from the trees, plants and flowers is her for us to enjoy and to resonate with. Take the time to go camping often; visit the ocean and walk on the sand. Climb the mountains and run on the green grass in the meadows, go for a walk in the woods, experience nature. Notice the birds, go golfing, run, surf, swim whatever will get you out of the house to connect with the energy of the earth. While you are out in nature remember that there are nature spirits among us. Just as angels here to assist humanity the elementals are rooting for us as well!

The Seventh Spiritual Law
Honor Your Body

"There is no weight limit on beauty."
Danni Barreto

Honor yourself. Your life is a gift. It is an honor to be in the physical body and to have the breath of life in your lungs and blood running through your veins. You have been given the gift of experiencing life!

As a podcast host, I have interviewed many experts in their fields over the years.

I have interviewed more than one guest who has said that there are many souls waiting to come down to earth and have a chance to live in a human body. We often take our bodies for granted and forget how amazing we truly are.

Your body should be treated with love and care as it's how you get around in the world. It is imperative that you exercise, drink water, and get plenty of rest, this will reduce stress and anxiety and will help with your overall health. You are an energetic being having a human experience. Honor the body that is allowing you this amazing opportunity to experience life.

I suggest everyone listen to music often, sing, hum, dance. Music is healing. I believe we will eventually heal our bodies with sound, vibration. This is done today, and healing frequencies can be accessed online depending upon your ailment.

Many of us take our bodies for granted unit they begin to speak to us and give us the sign, the wakeup call that we are not treating it with love and care. You see we were meant to move around and most of our jobs today require us to sit. We do not get the amount of exercise that we should be in our daily activities.

Many people work out at the gym, walk, run, bike, hike, swim, play tennis, which changes your life. When you are active the weight comes off; eventually and you just feel better. You have a better attitude towards life, and you sleep better too.

I believe exercise is the cure for most anything that ails you. It's the act of getting up and getting moving. The more you move around, walk, jog just function the better our bodies like it. We get stiff and sluggish when we stop moving. The old saying is "a couch potato" but with all our electronics available today we can easily get stuck in the house at the computer or on the TV.

We all must become in tune with our own bodies. Being in tune means listening to your body. I know when my knee hurts, I start moving. The exercise releases the tension, and it stops hurting. It's amazing how the body talks to you.

We are a result of what we put into our bodies. If we do not eat properly our body alerts us immediately. You know what is good for you and what is not. When you consume food or drink that does not agree with you; change your eating habits. Lack of movement and the wrong foods going into your body can cause disease within the body. "We are what we eat "is a famous saying but is the absolute truth. What we put into our bodies is who and what we become.

You have a choice to eat fast food or go the grocery store and buy healthy meals and snacks. Now we all need to live a little so to satisfy your cravings; create a cheat day. Pick one day during the week that you can eat anything you want. This will cure the cravings and will not make a huge difference in your weight. Eat that piece of chocolate cake or a peanut butter cookie, cupcake, or candy. You can have anything you want but in moderation. Moderation is the key.

The medical industry has its pluses and its minuses. There has been great accomplishment in the medical industry in the past 25 years that has saved numerous lives.

Homeopathy medicine is also on the rise as many of people choose to take a natural approach to healing; and not just for themselves but for their pets.

Natural medicine has also grown tremendously in the West and has become a wonderful alternative to prescription medications.

Humanity is realizing the benefits of natural healing such as massage therapy, acupuncture, meditation, retraining the muscles in physical therapy. The Bach Flower Remedies are popular as aromatherapy and essential oil use grows in popularity now more than ever.

Faith is taking the first step even when you don't see the whole staircase."
Martin Luther King Jr

The Eighth Spiritual Laws
Have Faith, to Believe

Faith is believing in something that you cannot see and a clear knowing in your heart.

If you would like to communicate with your Guardian Angel, you must have faith.

Faith is knowing that there is a higher power that loves you and wants the best for you. Faith is believing the events that are occurring in your life are for your best and highest good. Having faith is also trusting yourself. This is not so easy as many of us do not trust ourselves. We often look for others to tell us what to do or to confirm our decisions. It is truly helpful to have a second opinion; but we should strive to have confidence in ourselves. Knowing that we are making the best choice for our highest good and connecting with your Angel for confirmation. I have learned that if it does not feel right then don't do it. Intuition and faith go hand in hand. We all have a built in knowing. It's up to us to choose to use our internal compass to navigate through life. Intuition is that gut feeling confirming what we know to be true. Our body does not lie. When you feel it in your soul, you know that you are correct. When we have faith in our feelings and go with them; the results are amazing. Take the leap of faith and go with your gut!

What you perceive to be a curse may be a blessing in disguise? Spirit/God and the Angelic realm work behind the scenes to create miracles we may not foresee coming. This is why it is imperative to have faith in Spirit/God and your Guardian Angel.

It is possible that you came down to earth to learn a specific life lesson and you are not cursed or unlucky, at all. You are learning, you are in earth school. The important thing is to know that you are never alone for the angels watch over you. Have faith that God, the Divine Source Energy knows what is best for us and loves us all unconditionally.

It is to your benefit to use your intuition in all aspects of your life. We all have intuition; it is our internal compass. And as they say, "Go with your gut feeling when making decisions."

Practice quieting your mind for a few minutes a day and the answers will come to you. We all get that gut feeling, the silent knowing that is there to guide us through life. The feeling is our intuitive knowing, our sense of direction to determine what is true, good, and proper and what is not.

Now faith is the assurance of things hoped for, the conviction of things not seen. Hebrews 11:1

When you are using your talent, your gifts, you will maintain a state of Balance. When you do what you love your life is blissful. This is very important for your health and wellbeing. We often lose our balance between work and play. It's key to maintain balance in your mind, throughout your body and in your soul. I suggest meditation, to quiet your mind. Plugging into Source energy, the Holy Spirit through meditation only takes a few moments and will quiet the mind and heal your soul. Connection with the energy of the Divine Source will calm you, energize you and balance your energy centers. Bringing in the light energy is like hitting that refresh button on your computer.

"A Grateful Heart is a Magnet for Miracles."
Unknown

The Ninth Spiritual Law
Be Grateful

The universe loves gratitude and so do the Angels. The universal energy picks up on our grateful energy. Your grateful vibration goes out into the universe and delivers blessings back to you. The more gratitude you send out the more gratitude you will receive, the universe blesses you. It's an amazing energetic system set up for our benefit. There is no room for error; it's all determined and coordinated by the energy you are sending out each day of your life. Many doors are open when you are in a grateful state of mind. Often, we must reprogram our thoughts and beliefs to come to a place of gratitude. To begin to look at life differently and be grateful for the small stuff. Living your life in a state of gratitude is a game changer. It is the small things in life that are what I have become the most grateful for. There are many homeless people who do not have a warm bed to sleep in, or shelter with a roof over their head to protect them from the elements. Many people need food to warm their stomachs and nourish their bodies. Taking a shower and having a clean toilet for many people is a luxury, which in this day in age it is hard to believe that people go without the basic necessities of life. Humanity has not taken care of its own and we need to begin. Interviewing guests who connect with the extraterrestrials is always an eyeopener on my show, but the one thing that has stuck in my mind is an interview I did where the guest conveyed that the ET's have said, "They do not understand why we don't take care of our own people." And I don't either. I believe that most people are grateful to receive a smile or a kind word from another human being. You never know when you are performing an act of kindness and who will benefit from your kind act. We must become kinder and more compassionate people who take care of our own brothers and sisters. Practicing gratitude is said to improve mental health and has proven to help relationships. Some people have a gratitude journal others say prayers to express their feelings of gratefulness. Gratitude is golden. Being grateful is a choice. It is interesting how the energy flows, when you begin to recognize what you're grateful for in your life everything changes for the better! When you recognize your blessings and are grateful, the result is joy and prosperity. You can look at life from a view of difficulty and hardship or you can look at life as a blessing and an adventure. The more blessings you are grateful for the more blessings come your way and the more grateful you become. So, take a moment or two daily and thank Spirit/God for what you have. Do not speak of what you don't have, be grateful for what you do have and know that with that grateful energy flowing out to the Universal will be making its way back to you. It's amazing how the universe works. The Universe picks up on whatever your vibration and energy field are sending out and responds accordingly. Knowing this law is key to working with Spirit/God and your Guardian angel.

The Tenth Spiritual Law
Be Aware of the Signs and Numbers

"Number rules the Universe"
Pythagoras

Angel numbers are a sign. Many people have heard of the 1111 phenomenon. And the buzz is true. When you begin to meditate and connect with Source Energy you begin to see the signs. 111 is one of the first signs you will see. Numbers have meaning and have held their own specific energy from the beginning of our universe. As time goes on and you continue to work on yourself you begin to see 222 and then 444 or 888. When you see 222 often, I feel like it's a progression as we evolve and raise our vibration to love and compassion, kindness and charity. Seeing the Angel number 222 repeatedly is your Guardian Angel encouraging you to remain positive and know that your angels are with you. The number two in numerology represents a pair, or a duo, or could signify a twin flame. The number two is also associated with partnerships and relationships. The numbers appeared in order when I began seeing them on a consistent basis and I do believe it works that way for all of us as we grow. The number 444 is one that comes up all the time and I know now that it is the Universe and the Angels confirming that you are on the right path. To me 444 means you are exactly where you are supposed to be, and the Universe is giving you a high five! Speaking of fives when you see 555 it is a sign of change and transformation. Many people are seeing 888 which means three eights in a row. It's abundance and prosperity. The number 888 is also associated with karma, what goes around comes back around. God used mathematical law to create the Universe. Numbers are our foundation. You may have heard that the Universe speaks in numbers and that is the absolute truth *The European Journal of Theology and Philosophy* (2022) stated that, Nikola Tesla believed that the numbers 3,6, and 9 hold the keys. He implied that they represent the higher dimensions. His theory was based on the concept that 3,6 and 9 are the most important digits. He was so obsessed with the number 3 he did everything in 3's. People are looking for answers and are finding guidance in the signs. Messages from Spirit/God the Angels and our Spirit Guides arrive in many forms, often in the form of birds. Cardinals and yellow birds will appear to people after a loved one has passed. It is a sign that they are moving on to their next adventure but want you to know they are alright. Crows call out when there is a message for you and butterflies are often loved ones passed who are fluttering by to say hello. The angels are always showing us signs, but it is up to us to pay attention. Last year I was traveling by myself and felt nervous at the hotel I was staying at. In the morning, I peeked out the window to see a car directly across from my window with a license plate that read:

The Angels are Here Watching Over You. I almost fell over, I mean this was a blatant sign, it could not have been plainer. I pulled out my camera and took a picture to remind myself of how awesome the angels are! The signs are all around us some come in numbers and others in words of a song, but it is up to us to pay attention to the signs that the Universe is sending us to guide us along our journey. Our deceased loved ones will come and visit us and give us signs that they are around. You may experience the smell of that person's perfume or cologne, and that is their way of letting you know they are with you. Songs are another sign that a loved one is trying to connect with you. A song that you used to sing together or remember from a time spent together. You may also receive pictures in your mind's eye of a person or a place, these are visual signs. The sign may also come in the form of a billboard as you're driving down the road. The important thing to remember is to pay attention to the signs and use your intuition. The signs are markers on our path in life to show us the way and to assure us we are on the right road. That is a question that people often ask me, if they are on the right path? The answer is of course you're always on the right path you may take a few detours along the way, but you will make it to your destination.

The Eleventh Spiritual Law
Do Not Judge Another

Judgment of each other must stop, as we are all souls with no idea what another person came here to learn and experience in this lifetime.
Nancy Yearout

Living in a material world is not very easy and people are judged by their appearance, clothing, car, position, home, and the list goes on. Unfortunately, much of humanity finds it difficult to practice nonjudgment. People see a person on the outside, but we don't take enough time to peer into the inside of each other. We seem to judge other people without even knowing who they are as a person at soul level. Once you become aware and look a little bit deeper, you begin to recognize the judgments you are making and the judgment that others are making of you, then this law is easy to follow.

Mathew 7:1–2
"Do not judge, or you too will be judged.[2] For in the same way you judge others, you will be judged, and with the measure you use, it will be measured to you.

Many of us get hung up on what something costs or how a person looks or dresses or what car they are driving. The material possessions trip people up every time with their attempt to keep up with friends and neighbors by buying the car or home that will look good to others and not being true to themselves. We have been programed to take into consideration what other people might think or say about our choices. Choices of career, lifestyle and even partners. I have witnessed a family rejecting a new spouse as they judged the new spouse unworthy to be in their family. Let's take a step back and know that objects can always be replaced but your health and people and animals cannot. Humanity must keep their priorities straight. Money, appearances or shiny things can't buy you fulfillment or love. The fulfillment that we are all looking for is the love we receive from connecting to the Divine Source, our creator, God. Your life will be filled with joy when you connect with the Source Energy. Do you really think it will matter when you are gone from the earth plane what kind of vehicle you drove or what outfit you wore or your hairstyle and Botox injections?

We are all souls having a human experience and know that we are all equal. We all arrive here with nothing, and we all leave here with nothing. What remains with us is the love in our hearts and compassion we shared while we were here. We keep the love forever! Our world has become extremely judgmental of each other. People judge you regarding your wealth, the color of your skin, hair color and type, your position, religious affiliation, where you live, what you drive, and where you go to dine. They do not see the inside of a person, what we stand for at soul level. People are obsessed with their looks and what others think of them, seeking approval from someone else's judgment from the outside is completely backwards. If we could stop judging each other and look at the soul instead of the body we would find peace.

We are here on the planet to learn and to evolve into kinder more loving people. It is up to each one of us to go within and work on ourselves. The jealousy comes from not feeling secure in your own skin. We all have issues from childhood and from living life that must be addressed for us to become whole. We cannot blame our parents or our caregivers or family for our issues. At some point we all must look at ourselves and deal with the shadow side of ourselves to grow. This my friend is not an easy task, none of us want to look at trauma from our past but it is releasing the energy of those emotions that free us to move forward and evolve. We are evolving at our own pace and that is exactly as it needs to be. Be the example for others as your light grows brighter.

Section Seven

Gabriel The Archangel's Letters to Humanity

"I am Gabriel, who stands in the presence of God, and I have been sent to speak to you and to bring you this good news." Luke 1:19

Gabriel is named in Hebrew tradition and is considered one of the highest-ranking angels in Judeo-Christian and Islamic religions. He and Michael are the only angels mentioned in the Old Testament. Archangel Gabriel and I have been communicating for a few years now. Another Angel communicator mentioned how I might bring him in to receive messages and I have been channeling his messages ever since. When I talk to Gabriel, it is like conversing with an old friend. When I ask him a question, he responds to me telepathically and tells me what to write down. For the messages that I channel for humanity, he dictates, and I write. This conversation first began with me asking him about my life as I was grieving over a divorce at the time. I knew right away this was not me responding as I don't speak as he does or write the way he dictates. I was surprised and delighted to be able to communicate with him. I am still amazed and surprised by the messages that he gives me to deliver today. Our relationship grew into me asking him if he had a message for the collective, for humanity, as there is much violence and unrest on our planet. Again, to my surprise and delight, he did. I was so taken aback by the messages that he was bringing forth that I began to read these words on my podcast and on my YouTube channel. I developed a page on my website but truly felt they needed to be put into book form for all to read. Today I am focused on the messages that he brings for humanity. Now here is a little history about St. Gabriel the messenger: Archangel Gabriel is an Archangel with the power to announce God's will to humans. He is mentioned in the Hebrew Bible, the New Testament, and the Quran. Archangel Gabriel is seen as both male and female. His name means "strong like God" or "God is my strength." He is often seen with peace lilies, trumpets, harps, or scrolls. He has many musical connections. I pick up a male energy when I am working with Gabriel. He is very patient with me as I write down his words to humanity on my pad of legal paper. I pick up a male energy when I am working with Gabriel. He is very patient with me as I write down his words to humanity on my pad of legal paper. St. Gabriel the Archangel appears at least four times in the Bible to bring forth messages from God. The following Bible passage comes from the McConaughey family Bible published in the late 1700's and reads completely differently from the current Biblical translations. Read for yourself:

> *As the Dedication of the English translation of the Bible to King James the First of England seems to be wholly for the purpose of edification, and perhaps on some accounts improper to be continued in an American edition, have substituted a short account of the translations of the Old and New Testaments from the original Hebrew and Greek in which they were written.*

There is quite a bit of editing in the Bibles of today. They have been translated from the original Hebrew and Greek languages to Latin and then to English and Spanish and more with editing of the translation changing the words and thus changing the intended meanings over time. The Bible that I am using for the following passage is more than 239 years old, but still a translation as you read above. This is somebody's interpretation of what God or Jesus, or the apostles said or intended to convey to humanity. We need to take all of this into consideration when reading the Holy Scripture. The following scriptures are taken from my family's Bible, dated in the late 1700s. Gabriel appears to Mary.

The Gospel according to St. Luke Chapter 1:26–37

26. *And in the sixth month the angel Gabriel was sent from God unto the city of Galilee, named Nazareth.*
27. *To a virgin espoused to a man whose name was Joseph, of the house of David; and the virgin's name was Mary.*
28. *And the angel came in unto her, and said Hail, though art highly favored, the Lord is with thee: blessed art thou among women.*
29. *And when she saw him, she was troubled at his saying, and cast in her mind what manner of salutation this should be.*
30. *And the angel said unto her, Fear not, Mary; for thou hast found favor with God.*
31. *And behold thou shalt conceive in the womb, and bring forth a son, and shalt call his name JESUS.*
32. *He shall be great and shall be called the son of the Highest: and the Lord God shall give unto him the throne of his father David.*
33. *And he shall reign over the house of Jacob forever; and of his kingdom there shall be no end.*
34. *Then Mary said unto the angel, how shall this be, seeing I know not a man?*
35. *And the angel answered and said unto her, The Holy Ghost shall come upon thee, and the power of the Highest shall overshadow thee; therefore, also that the holy thing which shall be born of thee shall be called the Son of God*
36. *And behold, thy cousin Elisabeth, she hath also conceived a son in her old age: and this is the sixth month with her who was called barren.*
37. *For with God nothing shall be impossible.*

38. And Mary said, Behold the handmaid of the Lord, be it unto me according to thy word. And the angel departed from her.

The Angels are God's helpers and are ready to assist us when we call on them. The Angels have come to my aid more than once. I was rescued in a snowstorm by a young man that pushed my car out of a snow drift and then disappeared into thin air. I have also had a woman show up at my door that I had forgotten to lock as a reminder to a single Mom with two little children. Often you encounter a person that may be an Angel assisting you without you realizing it until after the fact or at all. When you have things like this occur frequently, you begin to understand that you are not alone. You begin asking for assistance and receive it graciously. The Archangel Gabriel is also mentioned in the scripture as a messenger for God.

The angel said to him, "I am Gabriel. I stand in the presence of God, and I have been sent to speak to you and to tell you this good news." Gabriel is the angel that God sent to speak to the Virgin Mary. Luke 1: 19 reads

In the book of Daniel, verse 9: 21, Gabriel is described as a man. It is important to know that the Angel Gabriel interpreted Daniel's visions. One more interesting fact is that Gabriel is the angel that announced the birth of John the Baptist. Gabriel is truly God's messenger. You will find the messages from Gabriel on my website. The messages Gabriel brings forth are to help the collective as we shift into a new reality a new vibration. This is why Gabriel is bringing forth messages for me to deliver to humanity. These messages are what God wanted Gabriel to convey to you, his people. I began channeling Archangel Gabriel three years ago. I was going through a tough time, and he gave me advice, hope and comfort. This process has grown into messages for humanity to help all of us. These messages are in chronological order. I place all new ones on my website as I receive the words, he wants me to write. I write his words verbatim and do not change anything. It is my honor to bring forth St. Gabriel's words to you and my hope is that all people will read and hear his messages of hope and love for humanity and that they are uplifted and hopeful for our future as a people. I am honored to bring you the messages from Archangel Gabriel to humanity.

The Letters

Dear Nancy,

This is the beginning of new times, lighter times, easier times. After the dark comes the light. We are here to assist humanity in becoming lighter, kinder, nicer, sweeter, giving, loving and peaceful people. For this is how we will raise the vibration on the planet Earth. Know that all of this is divinely planned. All play a part in the whole. Know who you are, get to know thyself inside and outside to become one whole being of light.

Do not be afraid or mock those who come to assist the people of your planet, they come in peace and bring joy and love to the energetic field of light. Stop the judgment of one another, go forth with love in thy heart and do not hold onto anger, jealousy, or hate. There must be disaster to invoke the necessity of connection. We can help each other, and we may have no choice but to help each other. Within each soul is a drop of light, a part of God that is good. It is up to everyone to shine their light in the world. God bless.

Gabriel, Angel of life.

Dear Nancy,

Tell the people of the Earth that kindness is the key to elevation for your planet. Life begins innocent and free. You must remain as such. Your life's health is dependent upon your happiness. Your state of mind carries much weight when it comes to your physical stability.

Please be conscious of what I say as the vibration changes for each of you at different times. Feel blessed you are hearing these words, and you will have a new vision moving forward. Go forth and spread love.

Gabriel, Angel of the Light

Dear Nancy,

Tell the people to not be afraid. The believers will be spared. Trust in God, a higher source of energy. Always love and never hate. People can be cruel but do not hate them. They are not aware. Many are lost.

Gabriel

Dear Nancy,

Go forth and tell the people of the love that God has for each one of the humans. This is a time of great achievement on your planet. Those willing to step up and be with the one true God will triumph and become one with the Source. The Mighty I am. You will need to give and receive only loving thoughts and deeds to ascend to the next level of consciousness. Go forth and do just that, love thy self and thy neighbor regardless of the words and actions toward others. Only love will solve the problems you encounter. Stay hopeful.

Love, Gabriel

Dear Nancy,

Go forth and explain to the people that there are ways to decrease and thin out the earth's population. Do not be fooled by what you are being shown and told. It is quite the opposite.

There are many innocent lives at stake and people will perish if the world of compassionate people do not stand up and stop the violence. This is the beginning of unsettled times. A war of all wars to achieve monetary gain with no value to the thousands of lives that will be lost over greed and power. Look to the sun as it will grow dark. Pray for the women, men and children, animals and all life on this planet that will be affected by a few. Stay strong in knowing we are here helping. A host of Angels are here now to assist as the fighting goes on, send good thoughts, good energy and love out and you will receive the good loving energy back. The vibration of love will help.

Gabriel

I ask about the Ukrainian/Russian crisis at the present time. Here is the reply:

Dear Nancy,

What you are witnessing is a mere ruse, a false front of what is truly occurring in and around the world. Do not be fooled by what you see, rather go within yourself to understand the truth. Those who walk in the light of the Lord will not perish.

Be strong, be smart, be faithful to the Divine Source as the people of this planet are greatly loved and have not been forgotten.

Love, Gabriel

Dear Nancy,

Tell the people of the planet Earth to not fear what they are being shown. As not all of what you see is the truth. Revealing the actual picture will come down the road. For now, believe in love and know that you will learn from these times. Grow and elevate your souls as compassion and kindness become part of your life. Love will encompass this entire planet as we change our vibrations to ascend to a higher frequency of Love!

Gabriel

Dear Nancy,

Tell the people of the planet to not fear the scenes that are broadcast to them as some of this is not truth. Only down the road will they see the truth even as it has been in front of you for many years. Your time of love and light will happen on the Earth plane as you evolve to a new vibration of love. Please do not fear these times, look forward to easier times, lighter time, loving times on your planet.

Gabriel

Dear Nancy,

There is hate in the world that must be transmuted to love. The energy is what makes the world go round as you might say. The energy flows in such a way that when negativity is brought into the mix it changes the vibration for the whole collective. The way to change and transmute this vibration is pure love being sent out. The more people who choose love over fear the quicker the planet will transcend into a compassionate and loving space. Right now, entities, galactic however you refer to the extraterrestrials who are divine and holy cannot stand the low vibrational frequencies at present. Therefore, it is important you help humanity see the light, understand energy and how it all works. These facts have been hidden from humanity, the collective to control the earth for personal and financial gain and power!

People seem to want power to feed themselves but are feeding on negativity which will only bring sadness and loss to their souls.

Gabriel

Dear Nancy,

This is a message that the collective needs to understand. My job is to bring you these ideas so that people will look at life from a new and fresh perspective. Sometimes humanity gets caught up in small things and does not see the full picture.

I am asking humanity to look at life as a gift that has been given to all of you. Change how you see yourselves. Look at yourself and each other as miracles! Because you are. Every one of you holds the light of God within your heart. You know it is there. Some choose to see the light in others choose to ignore its love. When you realize you are a part of God's light it changes your perspective.

We above see your lights as you are pure energy. Energy of the universal creation of love. You were created with love and now it is time for each soul to be aware of that love and bring it into their lives. Each soul has a choice to choose love or fear and anger. As you grow, more will see the love, feel the love and be the love, elevating humanity's energy to a higher frequency vibration. This is coming. Be a part of the change.

Gabriel

Dear Nancy,

My message today is a global one for all to hear. The tension in the Middle East is growing and things seem to be heating up. people are not paying attention and are focusing on other events.

We in the angelic realm are surrounding the situation now to bring about a peaceful solution for all involved. The unrest is the negative energy that has almost become a large ball of destruction. The negativity is being transmuted to light as quickly as possible but it continues to come.

Now is the time for all of humanity to come to realize what is important in your world and to come from a place of peace and compassion for each other. Remember we are all one, we are connected, we come from God Source Energy which is pure love. Our goal is to assist humanity in bringing love and compassion to the forefront. To make love the #1 vibration on earth. That is all.

Love Gabriel

Dear Nancy,

Tell the people to not fear their future. The future is what we create. Every person has a choice to make and when they choose how their energy flows it will either raise the vibration for good or remain in hate and fear. The more people wake up and realize they create their own reality and can choose to love over fear the better we will be.

The masses are expected to be angered at this time and to create more hate and unrest. Do not fall into this trap. It will just keep the cycle going. This is the tipping point for your people in the United States to find truth or not. The world is watching. Please choose love and compassion. We are all one.

Love Gabriel

Dear Nancy,

My message is to be kind. Be kind to each other and be kind to yourselves. There is much fear and harsh rhetoric being spoken. When you speak kindly to others and about yourself that kind energy resonates out into your home, neighborhood, office, planet to the universe. Energy is alive and moves quickly and fluently and good energy brings in more goodness and love.

When you send love out to others, animals, plants, flowers to the universe you are creating a brighter joyful place which raises the frequency for all.

You must acknowledge that vibration, spoken, sung or musical impacts us all. We sing to maintain the vibration in the heavenly realms as well as harps and liars for the pitch necessary to maintain a high balanced field of vibration with sound.

Much love to humanity. Please love each other as you would yourself.

Love, Gabriel

Dear Nancy,

The message today is to love your neighbors, friends, and family for who they are. In life you cannot change others, but you can change your reaction to any person's behavior. By changing how you react with people you change them too. Love is the strongest vibration in the universe and when you approach every situation with people with a loving heart the energy response is love. When you send out the love vibration from your heart to another you have broken all barriers. All anyone of you are looking for is love.

Your love may come from a person or another human but when it comes you feel it in your soul. Love lasts forever and bonds of love cannot be broken even in death. The energy of love lives forever, it's what makes the universe whole.

Love, Gabriel

Dear Nancy,

Thank you for bringing these messages forth to humanity. The cause is large and many of you have chosen to brighten the light here on earth. Thank you to all who serve humanity and bring love and joy to your planet. The lights will get brighter and the love stronger as more of you ascend to a higher consciousness phase. This is not the time to fear but to believe the Divine Source who energizes us all with the light of love and truth.

Love, Gabriel

Dear Nancy,

The time is drawing near for much to collapse and be reborn. As certain structures crumble new ones will emerge. It's up to you to create heaven on earth, you have the imagination to create a beautiful utopia here where you stand. Begin creating what you deem. What you believe you create. That is all for now.

Love, Archangel Gabriel

Dear Nancy,

My message for humanity is to open your eyes and see what's going on around you. Do not turn a blind eye and pretend all is well. It is up to the bold and the brave to stand up for your rights. The world is at a tipping point, the more of you who believe in the Divine Source and have faith that all will be well then it will. The energy of your thoughts creates new realities. So, think happy thoughts! The more you can think in a positive manner the more you will change the energy to positive vibrations thus creating a kinder, happier existence for all. This can be what makes the difference in your ascension coming to the planet. The thoughts and words have vibrations, and you attract what you think about all day long. So, change your thoughts to love and peace and in turn love and peace will be yours.

Love, Archangel Gabriel

Dear Nancy,

My message for humanity is to stop the mental conflict that fear is bringing about. What you think matters. People are concerned about the future. They know that lies have been told and continue to surface. As humanity wakes up you will all begin to see the truth and a great rebellion will occur. Many who have been harmed physically by these lies will be at the forefront of the rebellion. Many of you remain blind only because you choose to.

Remaining blind to the present reality is harmful to all. Most of humanity must stand up for itself to invoke change. This is all.

Love, Archangel Gabriel

Angel Message

The message today is forgiveness. Forgive others as you do not understand their motives. Many of you are angry at friends or family members for words they have used, or actions taken. None of these harsh feelings serve you. When you forgive others, you become free to move on. You become lighter and kinder. We say lighten up! The biggest advice I can suggest is to forgive others and yourself.

Many times, we see human suffering caused by a mistake made or words said in anger, it is most important to forgive yourself, as mistakes are a part of learning. Your soul will be free when you forgive. Forgiveness is the key to freedom. Open the door with your key and forgive others.

Love, Gabriel

My Dearest Nancy,

Time seems to be drawing near as you see more fire and disaster on your planet. There is coming a time of closure when people will see the truth and have a choice to make. Humanity is at a crossroads. This is where some of you will move to the light and the others to the dark. A complete divide or separation of souls.

This is the time to change your heart to love and understanding, love for yourself and for all of humanity. The love vibration is strong and will change the vibration, the consciousness and the attitudes of people moving forward. The love vibration will and does bring about peace. The light is associated with this vibration as everything is energetically connected to Source Energy. The direct connection to love is from your heart to God-Source Energy-The Radiant One.

Love, Gabriel

Dear Nancy,

The message today may seem harsh, but people are not standing up for their rights. It is important for all of humanity to stand together as one. There are a few who are attempting to control the masses. If you don't stand up for yourselves now all could go South as you might say. The lies are getting more evident so the more of you who decide to stand for truth and justice and compassion for your fellow man will thrive. There is a great divide among you and the gap must narrow. We ask you to begin hearing each other and listening to the words and thoughts behind them. This is the time to come together to create common ground and move forward for the common good of all mankind not just a few. That's all.

Love, Gabriel

Dear Nancy,

Great to be with you. I have been watching over many on the earth who are struggling with the violence that is occurring on your plane as of late. The storms in particular have caused much agony and stress among the people of these lands. Their loved ones have perished, and grief is hitting them hard in the heart and soul. Loss is a difficult emotion to feel and yet you are many who feel this emotion to understand life. I have comforting words to say to those who have lost a loved one, and that is that they are not gone, only moved to a new place to continue their growth. The love you shared shall be forever. Never to leave you. You are eternal beings here to learn lessons about life which are not always pleasant. Times are shaky, meaning that much must break down before the news can arrive. As the change occurs you will feel a shift in consciousness. There are many here right now who are experiencing the changes on your planet. Remember the shift will be a positive shift for all who stand strong in the light of love.

Love, Gabriel, Your Angel

Dearest Nancy,

There is so much going on to talk about today. The people are waking up to what is the truth. You are seeing the truth in plain sight. Pay attention to what is happening all around you. As more people see the truth the violence will cease. You may not see it soon, but it will come to pass.

Many young people are confused and believe information that does not contain fact. It is up to you and light workers to tell the truth of what is occurring so that others believe. The light never hides the truth.

Many souls have left after war and natural disasters on your planet. Many mourn their loved ones. Tell them that we the angels are with their family and friends in the Heavenly Realms. Blessing to all.

Love, Gabriel, Your Angel

Dearest Nancy,

The information I am giving you today is very important. Many of you are waiting for someone to save you but you must rise up and save yourselves. The people who are in charge are not revealing the truth concerning conflicts in your world. They neglect to tell you important details that you would not agree with. It is important for you to use your voice and not wander like sheep. This is the time to voice your thoughts and opinions as you are molding a world for your children and grandchildren. What do you what do you want to leave for future generations? This is not the time to sit back and wait for someone else to make a difference, change. Please hear these words the many lives will be saved if you speak up and say not to the falsehoods placed on you now. Connect with God and know we the angels are here to help all.

Love, Gabriel, Your Angel

Dearest Nancy,

As the world gets more involved in conflict it is up to everyone to voice his or her own opinion about the events occurring now. Please realize that the more voices that cry out the quicker the fear, anger and violence will stop. Your voices are powerful and if you band together can stop anything that is not beneficial for humanity. There are those who will hide the truth but as these truths are revealed more voices will be heard. Do not think your voices are unimportant as all who speak up will reap the reward of truth and freedom. This is a great time to know your worth. Your value is high as every soul is a piece of the Divine Source Energy. Together your energy is strong and powerful and that is what those in charge fear. Unite and conquer the lies and live freely on a new earth. plain full of love; peace and harmony.

Love, Gabriel, Your Angel

Dearest Nancy,

It is such a joy to see you and others bringing joy to the world with light and holiday spirit as you call it. Hearts are lighter at this time of year. People begin to think of what they can give their loved ones as gifts. The mere thought of you deciding to give changes the mood. This time of year, miracles occur because people slow down and enjoy time with their family and friends. Lots of cheer to spread over the next days. Merriment changes the mood and affects all of us.

Remember the elderly as they love a visit and a smile. There are many who are less fortunate as yourselves so remember to give to the kids and food for the families. Love is the most powerful force on the planet you live on and the more love you spread to each other the more pleasant your own life becomes. That is all for now.

Love, Gabriel

Dearest Nancy,

I am here to give humanity hope for their future. The good, the light of the Holy one shines bright, and more people are seeing the light and the truth. Many have been led astray and have conflict within themselves that must be tamed. With all things that happen in life but that is how we learn. I say we as we are all one from source. We are not separate. Humans have created such a separation. Connection is not how you feel loved and comforted. People are more comfortable when another person is kind and loving to them, comforting.

Each person has something special to add, this is how community is built with love, care, and stability. Love is the foundation. My message today is short but impactful as you all must understand how to connect to one another for love, warmth, and fulfillment. The joy of a group, the power of many together creates a powerful energetic frequency of love and connection for all of humanity.

Love, Gabriel

Dearest Nancy,

The cold has come to your place and the trees are losing their leaves. It is a time of death and rebirth for all of humanity. Now is a time of endings as the people of your planet see the untruths that have been applied to their lives. So many untruths you would have to be blind not to see, but even the blind see the truth through their senses.

There will be endings before the rebirth of a new way of being. Do not fear the new. The old must be discarded before the new can come in. The situation on your planet requires much assistance from the angelic realms currently but know we are with all who need us and ask for our help. We love all of you as our creator source does as we are all connected. We are all family. Love one another and go in peace.

Love, Gabriel

Dearest Nancy,

Tell the people that now is the time to open their eyes and ears and see and hear what's occurring on your planet. The dark is doing everything it can to disrupt and cause destruction. This is global. Please stay in love and not fear. The fear energy is what drives and feeds the dark. Bring up your vibration to a higher level of compassion, kindness, forgiveness, and non-judgment. These are the qualities and energies that elevate and change the vibration to good. More and more people will be hurt by the darkness that is attempting to control the population unless you band together and rise! Stand up for the beliefs you know are true. This is a turning point for all of humanity be able to say no to destruction, hate and fear, the abuse and tragedy brought about by a few with a single agenda. Stand together. Love your brother and your sister for who they are, a part of God, a part of the divine creator. The spark is in each of you. Ignite the spark.

Love, Gabriel

Dearest Nancy,

Humanity is at a crossroads. The next few years will change things for the collective. You will grow as a people and achieve a higher state of vibration after the wars cease. You will discover that the fighting was not what you had been told it was about. Humanity is waking up to the lies of a few who have affected the many. Good will come out of all the chaos you see. It's not at all hopeless for you to see the light is peeking through and will become brighter and brighter. People don't want war and conflict, destruction, and crime. The vibration is already beginning to shift. Blessings to all.

Gabriel

Hello Nancy,

It is the top of your New Year as you say so happy, happy New Year to you on this January day. The angels are working to create peace on your earth. They work in groups and as individuals. They request that you tell humanity to ask for their assistance if needed and know they will be guided and blessed by their wings of light. The light is healing and brings joy and laughter into humanity's view. There are many lights shining bright as more of you see the truth and connect with the God energy, the love grows.

Love heals all and will bring about peace to your people. We are here to help bring about love, compassion, and kindness as you grow. all of humanity is growing at a rapid pace and will bring about more peace to your planet.

Blessings to all, Gabriel

Dear Nancy,

Hello from Spirit! The love is flowing more and more in your world! I see compassion returning as the alternative is unacceptable to your people. Truths are coming to light and people are changing their views. The veil is thinning between the worlds as love comes back into your lives. When you arrived, you brought the love with you and kept it locked in your heart and soul. It is time to open the heart and soul and let the love flow. as more hearts open the world will shift for you. This is all for now.

Love you.
Gabriel

Archangel Gabriel's Closing
Message to Humanity

Dearest Nancy,

We have been together for a long time and I am now accepting the fact that humanity is growing at a rapid pace and will begin to accelerate at a rate that was not expected by anyone including me. This advance will be great and will uplift the people to a new level of consciousness. One where the colors will be brighter, and your music will sound better than ever before. Everything will be heightened as you will be heightened to a new vibration and reality. This new reality will bring much joy to your people and fields of grass will grow and wildflowers will flourish. The planet is adjusting as you adjust to a new vibrational sequence. This advance in technology will lesson as humanity realizes the harm it is doing in general. New more natural advances will be made that benefit not only humanity but the planet as well. Mother Earth is reaching a new shift herself and as this occurs the weather on your planet will be affected. Some of the weather changes are manmade but I am referring to Mother Nature shifting in a natural way of growth. Nothing remains the same the energy is always moving and shifting and creating new. Stay connected to the Divine Source of Light and Love and know that we angels are always with you. Pray often and be grateful to be alive as this is a wonderful time for you. Please ask the angels for help as they cannot help you unless you ask them. You all have the freedom to ask for assistance at any time and the angels will always be there to guide you, love you and comfort you when needed. My mission is to bring forth the messages of God to the people so they may know that the divine Source Energy is here for them to connect to. Love each other and love Source God, the radiant one of light and the light will shine down on you.

Love, Gabriel

Angelic Advice

Have Fun! Attend a Rock concert, Country, and Pop concert, sing along and experience the music. Music is full of energy and vibration.

Experience the vibration of the music and the roar of the crowd at a hockey game or a football stadium.

See a Ballet, a Broadway play at the theatre. Visit a Jazz Club and listen to the music. Attend a Symphony. Go to a parade in a small town and stand with the people as the bands play and the floats drive by. Music can be uplifting and healing to the soul.

The right frequency will raise your vibration and balance your chakras, your energy fields. Humm, sing, dance, all are good techniques for balancing.

The Angels are Here to Help Us

There are thousands of angels all specializing in specific talents. So be specific when you ask for their help. If you need a wedding planner that is the Angel, you request. If you need a mechanic Angel that is the Angel team you request assistance from. Always be specific with your request and know that the universe gives us exactly what we request or something even better! Have you ever had someone show up to help you out of a bad situation and then they were gone, never to be seen again? And you wonder was that an angel? This sort of event has happened to me and others that I have spoken to.

Here's what happened to me. I was leaving work late one cold and snowy evening. As I was pulling out my office parking lot on to the main road my car got stuck in the snow. My car was halfway in the road and halfway in the parking lot. Now what was I going to do? Suddenly out of nowhere a young man appeared. He just showed up. I mean he came out of nowhere in the middle of the snowstorm and pushed my car out of the snow drift. He was tall and thin with a short haircut. He wore a black over coat and leather gloves to match. After he pushed me out, I turned to thank him, and he was already gone just as quickly as he had appeared. Angels are always with you and available to help you when you need them. You just need to make a request and believe. It's important to acknowledge the help they give to you and always thank them. Gratitude is very important energy and the Angels love gratitude too.

Do you remember who you were before the world told you who you should be? Self-knowledge is life changing. It's the foundation for a better life. It is important to know your own feelings, emotions, your strengths, and your goals, what makes you joyful and shine!

It's important for our mental health to Slow down and smell the coffee and the roses. It is the little things in life that you will treasure the most when you're older. It is important to still your mind. Take a few minutes out of your busy day and turn off your phone!

The peace we feel within, and true Joy comes from the divine source, God. As a spark of the divine is all of us we can carry that light here on the planet. We can choose kindness to others and to be kind to the animals. as they are energetic souls in their form. Be respectful of others. Be respectful of yourself. Love yourself and take care of you. If you do not respect yourself, you will not be able to respect to others. it is important to respect all of humanity whether you agree with their views and opinions expressed.

My Hope for Humanity

Today I know my life's mission here is to serve the Almighty and tell people how to connect people with Spirit/God. We all have been given the gift of free will, so I share my experiences with you and lead by example. Connecting with God, the Divine Source Energy has changed my life for the better in all aspects, body, mind, and spirit.

Connecting with Jesus and Mary has enhanced my life but connecting to my Angel has made me believe in miracles.

These experiences have shown me how the universe works and how we as humans have not been taught how powerful we are. We have been programmed to think we are limited in our capabilities, but the universe is infinite, and we can create whatever we desire.

The Angels recommend meditation on a regular basis, to regenerate your light body and for balance. Remember we have energy centers that spin. connecting to Source Energy, plugging in to the healing loving vibration above will regenerate you daily. Meditation can take on many forms, some people a walk in nature, a run, or yoga. The idea is to do whatever works for you. When you slow down and quiet the busy mind you are recharging physically, energetical and spiritually. When we connect to the Divine Source Energy, we gain wisdom and often a new perspective.

You may have heard this before but it is crucial to know that you are loved by our God/Divine Source, some say the radiant one. I believe and feel strongly that there is a father and a mother creator who love us all unconditionally. This is a powerful living vibration of love and light energy that keep you in full charge. However, you must plug in.

They love us so much that they have sent the Angelic helpers and spirit guides from the higher realms to assist us on our journey in life. Make your request, ask the universe for what you desire, have an open mind with pure intentions and belief. The universal powers that be will deliver what you ask for or something better!

Be independent! Do not rely on anyone else to make your decisions for you, this is your life. Be self-reliant. Women especially have been reliant.

Lord loves righteousness and justice; the earth is full of his unfailing love. Psalm 33:5 NIV Bible

Music changes our mood as the vibration resonates with our energy fields and naturally balances us. Music is my savior when it comes to working out, I love to hear my favorite tunes when I am on my bike or the elliptical. Now I will say that singing and humming is extremely therapeutic and should be done daily by everyone. Music is healing to the heart and soul. Now that you understand how Spiritual Law works, you understand that Whatever vibration you send out comes back to you like a boomerang. Be truthful in everything you do and

Be truthful in with your words and deeds.

Be honest when dealing with others and be honest with yourself. When you cheat it comes back to you energetically tenfold!

What you do in your life matters. How you treat others matters. Doing nothing is not acceptable. You must participate in your own way and do your very best for your soul. The Angels are our guides and our helpers. They are God's, Divine Source messenger and ours too if we choose to communicate with them. We have been disconnected for so long it seems odd for me to have to explain to people how to connect to the Angel that is standing right next to them, but this spiritual connection has been lost. It is my intention to reconnect you with your Angel now.

To be free you must stand on your own two feet, stand strong and let your intuition guide you. We all have a specific talent to make our way in life. Use your gifts. Each of us has a specific talent, a gift that is unique only to us to contribute to humanity. Another way that people's energy fields are healed is by the vibrations of music, the harp particularly. It is believed that when music is played on the harp the vibrations of the harp strings go into the body and balance the ill person's frequencies. Carrol McLaughlin, an award-winning professor, and healer oversaw one of the largest harp departments in the world. The renowned concert harpist explained that when someone has an area of weakness in their body, it means that it's not vibrating at its full frequency. As part of the research project, she conducted a healing experiment at a hospital's ICU unit. She played her harp for several patients. The result was a 27% reduction in pain without any change in their medications. It has been documented that she played for a man in a coma and after seven minutes he took off his breathing mask and said, "thank you". Another patient was ready to go into hospice but after hearing her play the music, his doctor canceled the plans as the patient's vital signs had improved dramatically. This comes from Harp Therapy International (harptherapyinternational.com). There is an International Harp Therapy program that trains and certifies its practitioners to heal with the harp. Now that's amazing! This demonstrates the miraculous healing that occurs when your frequency is put back into balance. Music is healing to the heart and soul. I know that when I listen to an upbeat song on the radio it makes me feel energized and happy. Shelly Snow, PhD, says: "The human voice has a remarkable ability to improve our health and well-being in ways that are not widely known." The vibrations of music have been healing us for centuries and continues to do so today. The harp is mentioned in the Bible 66 times reminding us of the powerful vibration of music.

Sing joyfully to the Lord, you are righteous; it is fitting for the upright to praise him. Praise the Lord with the harp; make music to him on the ten-stringed lyre. Sing him new song, play skillfully, and shout for joy. For the word of the Lord is right and true; he is faithful in all he does. Psalm 33: 1–5

You now connected to the Angels of Light!
May your connection to your Guardian Angel bring you comfort and joy!

Congratulations! You have earned your wings.

Love Nancy

About the Author

Nancy Yearout is a public speaker, an author, a psychic, an energy healer, and an angel communicator. She is the host of "Nancy's Psychic View" Taking the High Road to Humanity. Nancy Yearout is the voice of *The High Road to Humanity* Podcast and Video Talk Show. Nancy's video presence can be found on her YouTube channel, "Nancy's Psychic View." She is the author of, *Wake Up! The Universe Is Speaking to You*, focusing on energy and spiritual law. As a psychic empath and angel communicator she channels Archangel Gabriel's messages for humanity found on her website NancyYearout.com. Her gifts include claircognizance (clear knowing), clairsentience (clear physical feeling), and clairsalience (clear smelling), and some clairvoyance (clear seeing). As a light worker for the Divine Source, she aspires to bring forth love and light to the world with her words of wisdom. Her former career was as a successful Real Estate Broker and owner of her own real estate company practicing in New Mexico. Today she uses her platform to speak about Spiritual Law, the Divine Source, God, and the angels bringing forth truth to humanity. She is a messenger connecting us to our Divine Source Energy. The energy of love. She has two daughters, three grandchildren, and two cats and makes her home in Arizona.

My book; Wake Up! The Universe is Speaking to You is currently available, and I am proud to say has helped many people. The information is relative to the times we are living in now. It would be helpful to understand how the energy flows, how the universe works, and what is happening right now on our planet for many who are just waking up. In the book I touch on many aspects of energy and consciousness for a newbie who has no idea about this stuff. It's a nice introduction to spirituality with Biblical references and famous quotes throughout to emphasize the subject matter.

From the Author

Thank you for purchasing A Guide to Angel Connection Suing Spiritual Law, An Angels Connection to God. My hope is that you will connect with God/Spirit and your own Guardian Angel. Please feel free to add your review on your favorite online site. So, if you would like to connect with my events and upcoming classes and books, please visit my website NancyYearout.com.

The Author

References

All but one quotation, unless otherwise indicated, are taken form the Holy Bible, International Version, NIV Copyright 1973,1078,1984, 2001 by Biblica Inc. The "NIV" and New International Version are trademarks registered in the United States Patent and Trademark Office by Biblica, Inc.

Section Six Gabriel's Messages – Scriptures from the King James Version printed in English in the late 1700's.

Section Seven; My Hope for Humanity; Harp Therapy international accessed December 2023 harptherapyinternational.com

Section Canadian researcher by the name of Francis Nixon was a pioneer in the study of Vivaxis,

6TH
BOOKS

ALL THINGS PARANORMAL

Investigations, explanations and deliberations on the
paranormal, supernatural, explainable or unexplainable.
6th Books seeks to give answers while nourishing the soul:
whether making use of the scientific model or anecdotal and
fun, but always beautifully written.
Titles cover everything within parapsychology: how to,
lifestyles, alternative medicine, beliefs, myths and theories.
If you have enjoyed this book, why not tell other readers by
posting a review on your preferred book site?

Recent bestsellers from 6th Books are:

The Scars of Eden
Paul Wallis
How do we distinguish between our ancestors' ideas of
God and close encounters of an extraterrestrial kind?
Paperback: 978-1-78904-852-0 ebook: 978-1-78904-853-7

The Afterlife Unveiled
What the dead are telling us about their world!
Stafford Betty
What happens after we die? Spirits speaking through
mediums know, and they want us to know.
This book unveils their world…
Paperback: 978-1-84694-496-3 ebook: 978-1-84694-926-5

Harvest: The True Story of Alien Abduction
G.L. Davies
G.L. Davies's most-terrifying investigation yet reveals one
woman's terrifying ordeal of alien visitation, nightmarish
visions and a prophecy of destruction on a scale never
before seen in Pembrokeshire's peaceful history.
Paperback: 978-1-78904-385-3 ebook: 978-1-78904-386-0

Wisdom from the Spirit World
Carole J. Obley
What can those in spirit teach us about the enduring bond
of love, the immense power of forgiveness, discovering our
life's purpose and finding peace in a frantic world?
Paperback: 978-1-78904-302-0 ebook: 978-1-78904-303-7

A Little Bigfoot: On the Hunt in Sumatra
Pat Spain
Pat Spain lost a layer of skin, pulled leeches off his nether regions, and was violated by an Orangutan for this book.
Paperback: 978-1-78904-605-2 ebook: 978-1-78904-606-9

Astral Projection Made Easy
and overcoming the fear of death
Stephanie June Sorrell
From the popular Made Easy series, Astral Projection Made Easy helps to eliminate the fear of death through discussion of life beyond the physical body.
Paperback: 978-1-84694-611-0 ebook: 978-1-78099-225-9

Haunted: Horror of Haverfordwest
G.L. Davies
Blissful beginnings for a young couple turn into a nightmare after purchasing their dream home in Wales in 1989.
Paperback: 978-1-78535-843-2 ebook: 978-1-78535-844-9

Readers of ebooks can buy or view any of these bestsellers by clicking on the live link in the title. Most titles are published in paperback and as an ebook. Paperbacks are available in traditional bookshops. Both print and ebook formats are available online.

Find more titles and sign up to our readers' newsletter at
www.6th-books.com

Join the 6th books Facebook group at
6th Books The world of the Paranormal